Getting into Character

Getting into Character

Seven Secrets a Novelist Can
Learn from Actors

Brandilyn Collins

John Wiley & Sons, Inc.

Published by John Wiley & Sons, Inc., New York
Published simultaneously in Canada

Permissions to reprint previously published material may be found on pages 211–212.

This publication is designed to provide accurate and authoritative information in regard to the subject matter covered. It is sold with the understanding that the publisher is not engaged in rendering professional services. If professional advice or other expert assistance is required, the services of a competent professional person should be sought.

Library of Congress Cataloging-in-Publication Data:

Collins, Brandilyn.
   Getting into character : seven secrets a novelist can learn from actors / Brandilyn Collins.
      p. cm.
      ISBN 0-471-05894-7 (pbk. : alk. paper)
      1. Fiction—Technique. 2. Characters and characteristics in literature. 3. Acting.
   I. Title.

PN3383.C4 C65 2002
808.3—dc21   2001046894

Printed in the United States of America

10 9 8 7 6 5 4 3 2 1

Dedicated to Jane Jordan Browne,
literary agent extraordinaire.
Because of you, the world
is a better place in which to read.

Contents

Acknowledgments

Many thanks to my editor, Chip Rossetti, who was always so patient, and who never ceased to amaze me with his insights and skills. Lots of gratitude also to the sales and marketing folks at John Wiley & Sons, Inc.

And thanks, as always, to my agent, Jane Jordan Browne, and her staff at Multimedia Product Development. Multimedia associate Jeff Essmann, with his uniquely blended knowledge of acting and writing, made this a better book from day one.

Why Should a Novelist Care about Method Acting?

[The artist's] job is not to present merely the external life of his character. He must fit his own human qualities to the life of this other person, and pour into it all of his own soul. The fundamental aim of our art is the creation of this inner life of a human spirit, and its expression in an artistic form.

— Constantin Stanislavsky in *An Actor Prepares*

The "secrets" or characterization techniques discussed in this book can open a whole new world of thinking for you as a novelist. These techniques have been adapted for your use from the "System" or "Method" of acting attributed to the great Russian actor and director Constantin Stanislavsky (1863–1938). Today, the term "Method acting," which refers to the use of his techniques, has become part of our general vocabulary, although many have a distorted idea of what Method acting really is.

Stanislavsky never claimed to have invented the techniques used in his Method. Rather, he sought to bring together acting concepts honed over the centuries and present them in a logical way. He wanted a clear break from the nineteenth-century *representational* style of acting, which was geared toward mere outward effect. Instead Stanislavsky aimed for the *presentational* style, which was based on

1

conveying psychological truth. He believed actors should develop such an intimate knowledge of the characters they play that they take on the characters' inner lives. Actors could achieve this only through discovering the characters' emotions and motivations. Without such intimate knowledge, Stanislavsky believed, acting would be merely movements and spoken lines—certainly not the embodiment of the life of the character. His worst criticism of an actor's portrayal was to say "I don't believe you."

That same criticism from a reader—"I don't believe you"—is just as harsh for us novelists. It's clear that Stanislavsky has much to teach writers of fiction. After all, we deal with the same issues that actors do. We, too, seek to create full-fledged characters with a deep sense of human truth, rather than cardboard representations.

Stanislavsky's "ABC" books on the Method (*An Actor Prepares, Building a Character,* and *Creating a Role*) are considered classics in the art of drama and are still available today. They provide very informative background reading for anyone interested in writing fiction. *Getting into Character* focuses on seven of the most sweeping and eye-opening techniques Stanislavsky covers in these books, presenting them in terms that can radically change the way you approach your characters and their relationship to your story. These secrets are equally helpful to the "plot-driven" and the "character-driven" novelist.

Whether we start with a story or with a character, let's face it—we writers of fiction are alike in one way. We're a mighty strange breed. We view the world differently. We walk around with voices and shadowy figures in our heads. We tend to stare out windows, mumble to ourselves. The Normals can't begin to understand us. Only our first cousins, the actors, can come close to matching our eccentricities. For we share the same goal: bringing characters to life.

In sharing this goal, we also share with actors the basic means of achieving it: observation. From the very first, actors are taught to *observe.* Like actors, we must be ardent students of human nature.

We must watch people, take mental notes, become armchair psychologists of human interaction. Neither actors nor novelists need ever be bored waiting in an airport. There is far too much going on around us. In voices, walks, postures, and facial expressions, actors and novelists alike find inspiration for portraying their characters.

From this point on, of course, our methods of bringing characters to life diverge. Actors portray characters on stage or on screen, their bodies and voices the tools of their trade. They have the advantage of *realization*—they are live people whom the audience can see and hear. Novelists create characters on paper, relying only on words. Our advantage is *imagination*, which can be every bit as effective, if properly activated in the minds of our readers.

This basic difference between writing and acting is the reason we have so much to learn from our cousins. For while we are often tempted to overuse words, *all actors have is action*. An actress can't turn to the audience in the middle of a play and explain her character's guilt complex. She must *show* it. All of us writers have heard over and over again: "Show, don't tell." Yet we've all read novels whose scenes are full of telling—the motivations are told, the emotions are told, even the action is told. No wonder we zip through the story unmoved, our souls unshaken.

Good fiction can be defined with "Five Cs": convincing characters caught in compelling conflict. As we look at seven secrets our actor cousins employ to create convincing characters, we won't delve into deep study of these techniques from an actor's point of view. Indeed, our cousins may smile at our layperson's approach to their skills. But we are focusing on our art, not theirs. Like thieves in the night, we'll snatch what nuggets of knowledge we can and flee to our own dens to hunker and grin over their use.

Ever struggled with these kinds of issues in your writing? If so, you'll find something in this book to treasure:

> My story is about three girls, but they
> all seem the same.   ⟶   *See Secret #1*

I struggle with writing about something
    I haven't experienced.   ⟶ *See Secret #7*

Sometimes my dialogue seems forced
    and shallow.   ⟶ *See Secret #3*

Readers can't always connect with my
    characters' emotions.   ⟶ *See Secret #5*

My hero isn't three-dimensional.
    He's too much of one thing.   ⟶ *See Secret #4*

Some of my scenes are boring.   ⟶ *See Secret #2*

My descriptions are long but still
    seem ineffective.   ⟶ *See Secret #6*

My characters' motivations aren't
    always clear.   ⟶ *See Secret #2*

I don't know how to use dialogue to
    further the conflict.   ⟶ *See Secret #3*

My characters repeat the same gestures
    from book to book.   ⟶ *See Secret #1*

Beginning and seasoned novelists alike can benefit from these techniques. If you're just starting to write fiction, a whole world lies waiting to be discovered. Read and learn all you can of the craft. This book will be but one part of your study. If you've written numerous novels, the techniques we discuss will stimulate your creativity by making you think in new ways. Some of them you may already use instinctively. But by familiarizing yourself with all seven techniques—and in some cases raising your knowledge of them from subconscious use to the conscious—you will be able to employ them more easily in troublesome scenes.

Here's a brief look at the acting secrets we'll adapt and how they can transform your writing.

Secret #1: Personalizing

An actor has only one body to portray many characters. How does he or she make each character unique? This becomes particularly challenging when two characters are similar in age, education, and breeding. We'll learn how to create a fresh, new individual each time through discovering the "inner values" or core truths that will drive a character's actions and desires.

Through personalizing, you can create characters so distinctive that their traits and mannerisms become a critical component of the plot itself.

Secret #2: Action Objectives

Hamlet's classic question "To be or not to be" is not the actor's focus. It's no coincidence that the root of the word "actor" is "act." We'll talk about why and how an actor determines scene by scene what his character wants to *do*. These objectives then give clear motivation for the character's actions.

This chapter will teach you how to give each character specific objectives—stated in the form of action verbs—that will provide believable motivation for movements and emotions within each scene and throughout the novel as a whole. These specific objectives pave the way for conflict, ensuring that scenes won't be merely setups for what's to come.

Secret #3: Subtexting

The last thing an actor wants is to sound as though she is merely reciting lines. To appear natural when speaking, an actor must first understand the character's motivation for saying the lines. This motivation is found in the subtext, or underlying meaning, of the words. Sometimes the lines themselves have little to do with what's actually being communicated. We'll take a look at how and when to write this kind of "subtexted" conversation. Using only five words of dialogue, we will write a scene between husband and wife that vividly portrays their abusive relationship.

Subtexting is the technique that every author needs to know in order to create dialogue that is rich in meaning while sounding natural, for in real life, this is the way people often converse.

Secret #4: Coloring Passions

A passion involves more than one emotion. For example, do you believe love consists of only one human emotion? Think again. Our acting cousins allow their audiences to glimpse moments of many different emotions—jealousy, anger, even hatred—which blend together to portray love. We'll explore the wildly different "colors" or feelings contained in any one human passion and how they apply to our characters.

The technique of coloring passions, more than any other, is the one that will help you create the three-dimensional characters all novelists seek.

Secret #5: Inner Rhythm

In order to live a part through believable action, an actor must listen to his own inner rhythm of emotions. Otherwise his movements will seem false, merely "acted" instead of real. Inner rhythm may have little to do with the character's surroundings. Externally, the scene may seem quiet, while inside, a character's anger or fear or uncertainty beats wildly. Using two different techniques, we'll discuss how you can "hear" the inner rhythm of your characters, which will then give rise to unique actions and responses.

Through the concept of inner rhythm, you will learn how to create action so vibrant with life that readers will feel your characters' emotions.

Secret #6: Restraint and Control

How an actor must fight the clutter of her own mannerisms! "No superfluous movement" is the goal, and to achieve this she must practice restraint and control of her actions. Only then does she become free to move solely in ways appropriate to her character. For novelists, restraint and control apply to words. Often we use too many. Other times we use the wrong ones. We'll look at specific writing techniques that will help you choose the words that best suit your character's actions.

Through restraint and control, you will learn how to use vivid verbs and adjectives that create a strong visual picture, and the technique of "sentence rhythm" to help create the aura of your scene.

Secret #7: Emotion Memory

An actor can portray any character, no matter how different that character is from the actor, by reliving his or her own past experiences and building upon those emotions. We'll see how well emotion memory works for us. Through reliving a seemingly insignificant act familiar to us all, within ten minutes you'll turn into a cold-blooded, calculating murderer.

Using your emotion memory, you can write about any character facing any circumstance. For there is no emotion or motivation known to man that you can't find within yourself.

Three important points before we forge ahead.

First, every character in your novel will not require the depth of inner development that these secrets present. Think of these techniques as more germane to your main characters and the important supporting characters—those whom the English author and critic E. M. Forster called "round" as opposed to "flat." In his book *Aspects of the Novel*, Forster defined flat characters as "constructed around a single idea or quality," while the round character is one who is "capable of surprising in a convincing way." In other words, a flat character represents one idea and does not change throughout the novel. The round character is one who adapts to circumstances, learns, improves. Flat characters are not necessarily bad—in fact, novels need them. One of their best functions is to help display the very roundness of more important characters. Unfortunately, too often our main characters, while needing the utmost roundness, manage the barest of curves. This is exactly what *Getting into Character* is all about: rounding the characters who drive our novels into three-dimensional personalities.

Second, if the definition of the "Actor's Technique" (found at the beginning of each chapter) sounds foreign and even scary, don't be dismayed. Remember, these definitions refer to the art of Method acting, unfamiliar to many of us. The "Novelist's Adaptation" and subsequent explanation will make it clear. But the chapters don't stop there. In order for you to best understand how to apply these secrets, each chapter includes example passages from classic and contemporary authors. These excerpts represent various ways in which the technique can be used. I urge you to read them carefully. Following the excerpts are "Exploration Points," which contain questions and answers designed to stimulate thinking about how the secret was employed in the examples and how it can be applied to your own characters.

Third, by the time you finish this book, you'll have covered an abundance of exercises and steps for the various secrets. And you might be tempted to think that with all the steps required to write just one scene's worth of action and dialogue, you'll never get anything written again. Not so. Absolutely not. The last thing I'd want is for this book to freeze up your writing.

I've dissected, listed, and labeled every element in these concepts so you can best understand them. But the good news is that the more familiar you become with these secrets, the easier they will be to use, requiring far less conscious, step-by-step precision on your part. In this sense, using these techniques is like driving a car. When you first learn to drive, you have to pay attention to every detail: where your hands should be on the wheel, how to watch for other cars, when to use the blinker. But after a while, these things become second nature. This doesn't mean you should ever settle back completely, letting all awareness slip as you drive. And sometimes in troublesome spots—in icy weather or hard, driving rain—you'll need to return to the conscious effort of driving safely. Still, most of the time driving doesn't require step-by-step concentration on your part. In the same way, as you learn these concepts, they will become second nature. You'll have to concentrate on their individual steps only when you run into a troublesome scene.

Enough introduction already. On with the secrets!

Personalizing

ACTOR'S TECHNIQUE:

As no two human beings are exactly alike, so every role is unique—a soul to be created that is distinctive and individual. Attributing mere general mannerisms to characters based on their age and social class will produce cutout dolls that may just as well be moved from play to play. Through discovering the inner character and from observing real life—how one person holds his head, how another walks or uses her hands—the actor must pull together a composite of mannerisms that creates the unique character being portrayed.

NOVELIST'S ADAPTATION:

The technique of *personalizing* each character is just as important in writing fiction as in acting. Without personalizing, we face the pitfalls of clichéd characters such as the "old man" or the "young woman." Our adaptation of personalizing focuses not on hair color and body type, but on the discovery of a character's inner values, which give rise to unique traits and mannerisms that will become an integral part of the story.

The Importance of Personalizing

"You can dress him up but you can't take him out."

"All dressed up and no place to go."

Ever heard those phrases? Their meaning is a little different, but they share a common thread. Both imply that outer accoutrements are less important than inner character and motivation.

Personalizing is absolutely critical for a novel. Yet many writers, especially new ones, have particular trouble with the concept of developing full-fledged characters. As noted in the Novelist's Adaptation, personalizing focuses not on physical attributes but rather on a character's inner values, which lead to traits and mannerisms. When we speak of "traits," we mean the general attitudes of your character, such as patience, arrogance, humility, selfishness. Traits define the basic personality of your character, just as we use traits to define people in real life. When we speak of "mannerisms," we mean specific movements of a character: the way he holds his head, the way she walks or talks, his facial expressions, and so on.

But how do we go about personalizing? And what can we learn from Method actors? The Method actor's secret to personalizing is based upon this principle:

> Personalized characters are built from the inside out.

In *Building a Character,* Stanislavsky notes that the most talented actors don't just assign traits and mannerisms to a character based on general facts about the person. Instead, these actors allow traits and mannerisms to grow of their own accord by first discovering the character's "right inner values." These inner values are the core truths of the character. They define the person's worldview; they drive his or her desires and actions.

For most novelists, Stanislavsky's approach is a radical idea. Instead of allowing ourselves to discover our characters' inner values, we have a tendency to characterize them on the outside—merely dressing the mannequin, so to speak—hoping somewhere along the way to discover a few inner truths about them. But too often, we don't go deep enough.

The trouble is, no matter how exciting our plot, how intriguing the action, or how great the danger, readers will fail to be caught up in the story unless they connect in some way with the characters. This connection is not superficial in the least; it links the reader's innermost being to the very soul of a character.

Two years ago, while I was on vacation at a lakeside resort, a mental image of a character popped into my head. I was minding my own business, ogling all the large boats along the docks, when this character invaded my thoughts. He was a young boy of about ten, a runaway, hungry and very alone. I "saw" him standing on the dock, head tilted back, watching a small group of people on a huge boat preparing to go out on the water. The longing this boy felt overwhelmed me until my own chest nearly burst from it. More than anything in the world, more than money in his pocket or food in his stomach, he wanted to be on the boat with those people. Only a few feet separated him from that boat, yet the distance may as well have been a canyon. He wanted to be up there not because his presence on that boat would convey access to wealth, but because he simply wanted to *belong*. Wanted it, yearned for it with all his might and strength. So close to people laughing and enjoying each other, yet so very far. So utterly alone.

This little boy caught my heart. We connected on a very deep level. Two years later I still wonder who he is and when he will fully reveal himself to me. To this day I couldn't tell you his traits or mannerisms. I'm not even certain what he looks like. These things aren't yet important. What *is* important is my knowledge of the inner value that most shapes this boy: belonging is more important to him than anything else in the world.

I must admit this is the only time such a vision of a character has happened to me. Usually I approach a novel with a basic plot and *then* discover the characters. Still, somewhere along the course of writing, they'll inevitably do something I hadn't planned. How exciting when that happens! But whether you start with a character or a plot in mind, ultimately it's the characters who will drive your story.

Unfortunately, not all our characters are as open about their inner values as this young boy was with me. Many at first tell us nothing but their physical appearance. That's okay; take whatever they'll give you. If a character shows herself to you, and she clearly stands five feet four inches tall with brown hair and green eyes, don't dismiss her. Welcome her, in fact. Invite her to curl up on the couch, tell you who she is. Only then will you begin to truly connect. Her appearance may attract you, but her inner values are what will make her compelling.

Now, let's search for those intriguing inner values of your character and see how they can give rise to a unique, personalized set of traits and mannerisms.

The Personalizing Process

Naturally, you'll have to begin at the beginning: learning the basic facts about your character. One of the ways authors do this is to "interview" the character.

Some authors have a very structured way of interviewing their characters, using a long list of questions regarding age, gender, likes, dislikes, background, education, family relationships, and so on. That's fine. Making a checklist of details is a good entry into the personalizing process and will dovetail with what we are trying to accomplish. In a moment we'll talk about where such an interview list will fit into the technique of personalizing.

Authors at the other end of the scale use a free-form method to get to know their characters, making notes as facts about them come to mind. Still other authors use techniques somewhere between the free-form and the structured interview. Whatever your method, you do need to discover the highlights of your character's background and experiences, for these will color the person's view of the world. But for true personalizing, remember this: *these facts about your char-*

acter will not be ends in themselves. In fact, they will be merely the beginning.

In a nutshell, here are the steps to the secret of personalizing. We'll go through each one to fully explain the process.

Step 1. Begin a line of questioning with your character and pursue it until you "hit bottom." Hitting bottom means you arrive at the "So what?"—or logical conclusion—of that line of questioning.

Step 2. The final "So what?" question will reveal a core truth or "inner value" about your character.

Step 3. In turn, this inner value will give rise to a trait.

Step 4. Then pursue this line of questioning even further to see if you can hit bottom a second time.

Step 5. If you can hit bottom again, you will discover a specific mannerism based on the inner value.

Now, how to start this questioning process?

If Stanislavsky were alive today and willing to teach us novelists, his questioning process would most likely be based on the three levels of characterization that he describes in *Building a Character.* At each of these levels a deeper probing of the character gives rise to more personalized traits, which in turn reveal specific mannerisms. Stanislavsky's disappointment lay in the fact that, amazingly, many actors stopped at Level A, and many others made it only to B. Yet only at Level C is true individualization reached.

All too often, novelists, like actors, tend to stop at Level B. We have understandable reason for doing so. Levels A and B aren't very difficult. We have one or two main characters in mind and a story to go with them, or perhaps we start with a story and figure out a couple of characters. Within the process of discovering our stories, we tend naturally to reach Level B. And then we think we have enough. The problem is, in this personalizing process, you will not conclude Step 1 and hit bottom with a line of questioning until you reach Level C. If you stop too soon, you'll miss discovering those valuable core truths about your character.

Level A: Division of characters into general categories such as socioeconomic level, age, gender, and career

Imagine the quick introduction of a game show contestant, and you've got Level A. "An English professor from Omaha with three children" or "A retired dog trainer who loves to fish." Getting your character to answer Level A's basic question of "Who are you?" is easy enough. Your character is a military man, a beautiful and wealthy woman, a homeless person, or an elderly gentleman. Any such category automatically brings to mind an array of potential mannerisms. In walking, for example, someone in the military may tend to march, while a beautiful and rich woman may strut, a home-less person listlessly amble, and an elderly gentleman shuffle. Or in eating, the military man may clear his plate with a quick deliberate-ness while the rich woman revels in the ambiance of fine food and etiquette. This level of characterization is of course necessary, and it's true that major divisions such as career and socioeconomic status begin to define a person. But we can easily imagine the stereotypical disasters we'll create by stopping here:

> an abused, abandoned romantic heroine = fearful, feels unworthy
>
> a detective who's clawed his way out of the slums = chip on his shoulder
>
> an elderly man with unrealized dreams = bitter, sour-faced

Let me hasten to add that the above aren't bad in themselves. Your detective from the slums may indeed have a chip on his shoul-der. The question is how to move him from mere stereotype to a unique persona.

Level B: Moving toward specifics

At this level we can begin to imagine some distinctions within a main category as we further define the character and how he or she fits into our story. You most likely will already know the answers to basic questions in Level B. For example, is your military man a private, a major, a general? Or is he in a specialized unit such as the Navy SEALs? Is the homeless person new to the streets or someone who's lived there a long time? In his working days, was the elderly gentleman employed in a factory or was he a high-level executive?

Answers to these queries will lead you to numerous lines of specific questioning. Let's say your story involving the military is about a young man who has just enlisted in the Marines. Perhaps he is following in the footsteps of both his father and grandfather. How will his family history affect his attitude toward the rigorous demands of the Marine Corps? Obviously, this young man's actions and outlook will not be based on the years of military training inherent to a general. But what if his grandfather was a general? After growing up hearing his grandfather's stories and learning at the old man's knee, might your character think he knows more than other new recruits? Might he approach his peers with a bit of a cocky attitude? Or might he have placed his grandfather on such a pedestal that he feels he can never begin to measure up?

Or let's say your character is that beautiful and wealthy woman. Is she newly rich or was she born into money? A character with new-found wealth may harbor a different attitude toward money than a woman who was born with a silver spoon in her mouth. If your story is about the homeless man, exactly how long has he been homeless? A man who's recently lost his job won't view the streets with the familiarity of a person who's been homeless for years.

Although at this level we are beginning to see some of the attitudes of our characters, the questioning up to this point only begins to scratch the surface. Therefore, any mannerisms or traits attached now will remain too generic. But it's just so doggone tempting to stop here. We figure we know the basic information about our characters, some of their perceptions of life, and we know the story or at least have a general idea of the story. Time to assign a few personality quirks and gestures and get on with the writing.

Not so fast. The fun begins at Level C.

Level #C: Personalizing of the character

At this level you will conclude Step 1 and move on to Steps 2 through 5 of the personalizing process. The character will become a unique person, with inner values and a resulting set of traits and mannerisms not duplicated in anyone else. If you employ an interview list, this is the level at which to ask the deeper questions that move you toward the core of your character. Obviously the answers to the first questions on your list—name, age, position, and so on—will already have been answered in Levels A and B. Your Level C list might include items such as: Was your childhood happy? Unhappy? Why? What are some defining moments in your life? What do you think of when you hear the word "mother"? How about "father"?

If you don't use a set list of interview questions for your characters, that's fine, too. You can still get to know your character by asking questions that naturally follow the answers you've received in Levels A and B. This is akin to the give-and-take conversation in making a new acquaintance in real life. That person tells you something; you respond with a question for more detail. You're told more, and you respond with yet another question.

For example, let's return to one of the characters mentioned above—the newly rich woman. Continuing the line of questioning you began in Level B, you might specifically ask: Would she view money as less important or more important than a woman who was born to it? Again, the trick is to play out each line of questioning until you hit bottom. Say you continue questioning your newly rich woman about her money, finding out just how important it is to her. You find it is indeed *very* important. You probe further along these lines. Is the money more important than friends? Family? How differently would she feel about herself if she didn't have money? *Very differently*, she admits; *my self-identity would be gone*. Gone? you repeat. *Afraid so*, she says. *I guess I define myself a lot by my wealth.* Aha! You've just hit bottom—the "So what?"—with this line of questioning (Step 2). You've discovered one of the core truths of your character: her self-worth is based not on who she is or what she's done, but what she *has*. This "inner value" lies at the very heart of your character and will drive many of her actions and desires.

On to Step 3. Now that you know your character bases her self-worth on her money, how will this inner value translate into outward attitudes? In other words, what trait will naturally result? Question your character further until this trait is revealed. You may discover she is proud, perhaps even given to bragging, about her wealth. Or perhaps you'll find that she is tightfisted, for if she ever lost her money, what would she be? The key here is not to leave this step until you understand how the inner value will directly affect your character's outward personality.

Once you've discovered the trait linked to your character's inner value, proceed to Step 4. Continue with the same line of questioning to see if you can hit bottom a second time. If you do, you'll discover one or more specific mannerisms tied to the inner value. For example, you might ask, with a self-worth based on money, what she has spent her money on. Probe this a bit. Let's say you discover she's bought herself a large diamond ring that she absolutely adores. She wears it all the time. This information has singled out her hands, putting you almost to a second bottom, but not quite yet. What else do you know about her hands? Is she proud of them? Are her fingers long and beautifully tapered or stubby and wrinkled? Perhaps she tells you they're not as attractive as she'd like, even though the nails are groomed and polished. This fact bothers her, and if it weren't for the ring, which is a sign of the wealth by which she defines herself, she wouldn't choose to draw attention to her hands.

Now you can ask her which of these two desires will supersede the other—her desire to avoid drawing attention to her hands or her desire to show off the ring? *Show off the ring,* she replies.

This is the second and final bottom of this line of questioning. At this point, you can proceed to personalizing Step 5. After all your probing, your knowledge of this character can now translate into specifics of how she will use her hands. She may talk with them, spread her fingers in graceful poses, rest them on the table at dinner rather than in her lap. Or she may have the mannerism of tapping a nail against her cheek as she's pondering something, or on a table when she's frustrated.

For another example of the personalizing process, let's return to the young Marine recruit whom we left in Level B. Say through questioning in Level C you discover that this young man feels he can never measure up to his father's and grandfather's expectations. You then might ask: What's his definition of measuring up? Perhaps he tells you that measuring up means a lifetime career in which he attains the rank of general, and it means upholding honor and integrity as expected of a strong Marine. That's a mighty lofty definition. You could probe more about how he formed it. What part came from his father? What part came from his grandfather? The character's responses might surprise you. For instance, the part about attaining the rank of general may not necessarily have come from the grandfather. You might ask about your character's relationships with these two men. To which man does he feel closer? Does he think he has more to prove to his father or grandfather? Where is his mother in all of this?

Let's say through all of this questioning you discover that your character has a difficult relationship with both men because of their constantly pushing him to achieve. The grandfather has always been dissatisfied with the performance of his own son, your character's father. And the grandfather has now placed some high expectations regarding honor and integrity firmly upon your character's shoulders. Further, your character's father seeks his own redemption in the old man's eyes through his son's accomplishments. The father is the one who has decided that the young man must become a general.

Now you are at the bottom of this line of questioning (Step 1). You can pose the "So what?" question. Ask the character: Which is more important, the showing of integrity or becoming a general? What if telling the truth about a certain situation meant that he would be passed over for a promotion? Which would he choose? Let's say the character answers: *If I knew I wouldn't be discovered, I'd lie rather than lose the chance for promotion, because if I can reach the rank of general, I'll prove myself both to my father and my grandfather.*

Aha—once again a major discovery! The character's answer has revealed an inner value (Step 2): External accomplishments pursued for the approval of two other people—his father and grandfather—are more important than personal integrity. Remember that this inner value will drive the character's emotions and actions.

You can now probe further to find what trait will result from this inner value (Step 3). Perhaps the young man will appear overly zealous in all he does, even to the point of being foolhardy, in order to achieve. Or perhaps he'll be just the opposite—reluctant and cautious because he fears failure.

Once you discover the trait, continue with the questioning to see if you can hit bottom again and reveal a specific mannerism (Steps 4 and 5). If the trait is that the character borders on foolhardiness in order to prove himself, you might ask: How does he handle nervous energy when he faces a challenge? Does he try to hide it so he can appear calm, cool, and collected? If so, how well does he

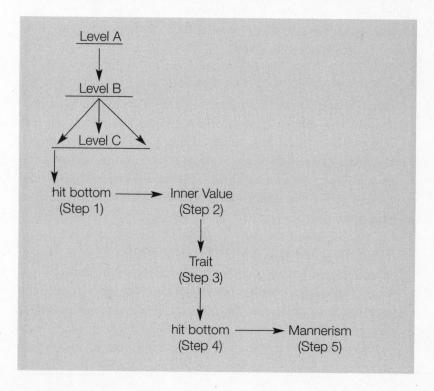

manage this? Even if he hides his nervousness well, is there a vulnerable part of his body to which the energy naturally flows? Perhaps he broke an arm by falling off a bicycle when he was too young to ride a two-wheeler—one of those early failures at trying to achieve for the sake of his father's approval. The memory still eats at him, and as a result, he unconsciously flexes that arm when he's nervous. Or perhaps his thumb twitches as a result of some other experience you uncover.

Once you've gone through all five personalizing steps with one line of questioning, start the process all over again by going back to Level B and picking up another line of questioning until you again hit bottom and discover another inner value. Then probe your character until you discover the resulting trait and mannerism(s). Continue your questioning in this way until you have discovered all the inner values, traits, and mannerisms of your character that you possibly can. Your character will then be a unique, personalized individual.

As you go through this process with your character, keep these three important points in mind:

1. *The personalizing process is not a one-shot deal.*

   You will find yourself returning to its steps again and again. No matter how diligently you follow the process, characters just don't reveal themselves all at once. As you write your novel, they'll hint at new facts about themselves, opening up new lines of questioning for you to follow. Take the time to go through the process again. No doubt you'll discover new truths about your character.

2. *Your character's inner values are not separate entities.*

   Sometimes they work together to produce resulting traits. Sometimes they mitigate each other. As an example, let's return to the newly rich woman with the inner value that her self-worth is tied to her money. This inner value could result in the trait of acting proud or even flaunting her wealth. However, as you pursue other lines of questioning, you might discover that she also possesses the inner value of placing the utmost importance on other people's approval. What will be the result of these two inner values working together? It depends on which one is stronger. If the need for approval is stronger, when this woman is with others who don't value or possess money as she does, she may tone down her flaunting in order to gain their approval. Or if she's with others who are wealthy, she may flaunt all the more to be accepted. (In Secret #4, "Coloring Passions," we will discuss in more detail how inner values work together to create the many different shades of a trait.)

3. *The personalizing process can work backward.*

Let's say right off the bat your character tells you he doesn't walk; he strides like a superhero on a mission. Don't respond, "No, no, I'm not supposed to know that yet." Instead, ask him why. Trace that mannerism back through the personalizing steps to the bottom of a line of questioning (Step 1), then work your way up that line of questioning from Level C to B to A. In other words, simply reverse the arrows on our chart. When you do this, one of two things will happen. Either you will discover the inner value that supports that superhero stride or you will find that you've misheard your character, for the truths you uncover will not support that manner of walking. In the latter case, be ruthless about tossing that stride aside, for if you insist on keeping it, you won't be true to the character.

This last point leads us to our next discussion—a more specific look at your character's mannerisms.

Putting the Spark of Life into Your Character's Mannerisms

Through the personalizing process, we've seen how you can discover the mannerisms based on your character's inner values. You have built your character from the inside out. You are now ready to put that final spark of life into your character's mannerisms. But first, two questions: Just how many mannerisms should your character have? And, does *every* mannerism have to be tied to an inner value?

As to the first question, no specific number of mannerisms for a character exists. Instead, use this general guideline: A character should display only as many mannerisms as are necessary to convey what is important about him or her without distracting from the story and the character's role within it.

You do not need to find mannerisms for every part of your character's body. Certain ones will appear as important. These will dominate and define your character. For example, one character may have a very distinctive walk, while another's walk is not distinctive enough to note. Or one may speak in a whiny voice while another's voice isn't particularly unusual. Don't fall into the trap of thinking that the more mannerisms your character has, the more defined he or she will be. The opposite is true. Too many mannerisms can lead to a "muddied" effect, just as too many colors blended together create a dull gray-brown. The *quality* of mannerisms is far more important than their *quantity*.

Some characters are more "colorful" in nature than others. These characters are fun, but you must be all the more careful not to overload them with mannerisms. Colorful characters typically aren't that way because they have *more* personalized traits, but because the personalized traits they do have tend to be extreme. "Over the top," we might say. A character loaded with too many over-the-top mannerisms will go from being pleasantly colorful to just plain unbelievable.

Now to the second question. Does every mannerism have to rise from an inner value? The definitive answer is "yes and no."

More mannerisms will rise from your character's inner values than you might think. Go through the personalizing process *first*. See what mannerisms your character displays to you. Then, as you get to know your character better and better in the process of writing your novel, you may find a certain mannerism creeping into his or her actions that was not a direct result of the personalizing process. However, since you've gone through the process and know your character well, this mannerism will likely be truthful to the character. The danger in clinging to this question's "no" answer lies in falling back into the habit of merely "dressing the mannequin." You want to avoid slapping on a hasty mannerism just because you think your character needs more.

As you discover your character's mannerisms, you'll want to infuse them with that final spark of life. The best way to do this is to draw ideas for moving, talking, walking, from the world around you. Watch people constantly. It's as simple—and as life-consuming—as that.

> Start a mannerism file, using the world around you.

The idea of observing others is nothing new to novelists. We pay it lip service all the time. But how often do we really put our people-watching skills to work? Often we become so busy *writing* that we forget to replenish ourselves with new, vital input. Where to gather these snippets of humanity? Everywhere. Watch people in cars, bars, and restaurants; in airports and buses and train stations; at work and at play; in stadium bleachers and church pews; at weddings and funerals; at dances, parties, school, stores; in their own homes and while traveling. Watch family, friends, and strangers alike. Watch yourself. Watch people standing in line, hailing a cab, yelling at another driver, hugging a loved one, laughing, eating, sitting, walking, talking, reacting. This constant observation of human nature simply can't be stressed enough.

A year ago I sat in a classroom trying desperately to push my right-brained mind into left-brained mode as the teacher lectured about aerodynamics and all manner of mathematical marvels involved in flight. But the student in front of me kept drawing my attention. He had the most interesting way of slouching in his seat, one shoulder raised to an uncanny level above the other, neck thrust forward and head held at an angle—somewhat like a hunchbacked bird listening for a worm. My fingers itched to write down that posture. How could I possibly concentrate on the teacher with this captivating sight before me?

We all need a way of recording such observations, no matter how facile our memories. Some authors carry small notepads or index cards for jotting things down on the spot. Others file observations away in their memories during the day, then write them in a journal at night.

In addition to watching people for mannerisms, don't forget other sources of ideas such as magazine pictures, voices over the phone or radio, characters in movies or plays, and descriptions in books. You can even glean ideas from animals and cartoon figures, adapting them to fit human nature. In one of the examples following this chapter, you'll see how a modern novelist uses a bear's hulking stance to describe a character.

You don't need to copy directly from these sources, and in some cases you shouldn't. But any one of them can springboard to that unique mannerism that is true to your character's inner values. Take a little here, a little there, blend, and create something new.

The result? A character who is vibrantly alive, whose facial expressions and movements reflect his or her core truths. A character that would please Stanislavsky himself.

Becoming More Familiar with the Process

When it comes right down to it, personalizing isn't all that difficult. It just takes time. We need to go through the steps carefully: questioning our characters to find an inner value, discovering the trait to which it leads, then discovering any specific mannerisms that may result. Unfortunately, many of us excel at only part of this process. We may have a great list of interview questions for our characters, but stop before putting the answers to their best and deepest use. Or we may boast an incredible mannerism collection gained through notes and pictures, but blithely sift through the pile, select a few, and slap them on our characters.

One of the best ways to completely familiarize yourself with the personalizing process is to personalize yourself. You might start at the beginning of the process and first discover your inner values, or you might start with a trait or mannerism and work your way backward. As you learn about yourself and how closely your own traits, mannerisms, and inner values are tied together, you'll better understand how effective this process can be in creating your characters.

Another interesting exercise in learning this process is to choose main characters from two different novels you have read—one character whom you felt was fully formed and believable, and another whom you found to be shallow. Then use the working backward technique to see how well their mannerisms and traits are tied to inner values that are clearly displayed through their actions. You will probably find that the trail of a believable character's mannerisms goes all the way back to the beginning of the personalizing process, while the trail of the shallow character's mannerisms leads nowhere.

The beauty of this personalizing secret is that the process creates the entire character, both inside and out. Still, this is only the beginning. In the following chapters, we'll see how the inner values and traits you've found through personalizing can lay the foundation for even further discoveries about your character.

 ## Study Samples

In these scenes we find examples of characters ranging from someone we might meet on the street to a more colorful type, both exemplified by only a few unique, personalized mannerisms.

FROM
David Copperfield
by Charles Dickens

Setting: England, mid-1800s. Dickens is known for his many colorful characters. Here we meet a shopkeeper as a down-and-out David Copperfield hopes to make a sale.

Into this shop, which was low and small, and which was darkened rather than lighted by a little window, overhung with clothes, and was descended into by some steps, I went with a palpitating heart; which was not relieved when an ugly man, with the lower part of his face all covered with a stubbly grey beard, rushed out of a dirty den behind it, and seized me by the hair of my head. He was a dreadful old man to look at, in a filthy flannel waistcoat, and smelling terribly of rum. His bedstead, covered with a tumbled and ragged piece of patchwork, was in the den he had come from, where another little window showed a prospect of more stinging-nettles, and a lame donkey.

"Oh, what do you want?" grinned this old man, in a fierce, monotonous whine. "Oh, my eyes and limbs, what do you want? Oh, my lungs and liver, what do you want? Oh, goroo, goroo!"

I was so much dismayed by these words, and particularly by the repetition of the last unknown one, which was a kind of rattle in his throat, that I could make no answer; here-upon the old man, still holding me by the hair, repeated:

"Oh, what do you want? Oh, my eyes and limbs, what do you want? Oh, my lungs and liver, what do you want? Oh, goroo!"—which he screwed out of himself, with an energy that made his eyes start in his head.

"I wanted to know," I said, trembling, "if you would buy a jacket."

"Oh, let's see the jacket!" cried the old man. "Oh, my heart on fire, show the jacket to us! Oh, my eyes and limbs, bring the jacket out!"

With that he took his trembling hands, which were like the claws of a great bird, out of my hair; and put on a pair of spectacles, not at all ornamental to his inflamed eyes.

"Oh, how much for the jacket?" cried the old man, after examining it. "Oh—goroo! How much for the jacket?"

"Half-a-crown," I answered, recovering myself.

"Oh, my lungs and liver," cried the old man, "no! Oh, my eyes, no! Oh, my limbs, no! Eighteenpence. Goroo!"

Every time he uttered this ejaculation, his eyes seemed

to be in danger of starting out; and every sentence he spoke, he delivered in a sort of tune, always exactly the same, and more like a gust of wind, which begins low, mounts up high, and falls again, than any other comparison I can find for it.

"Well," said I, glad to have closed the bargain, "I'll take eighteenpence."

"Oh, my liver!" cried the old man, throwing the jacket on a shelf. "Get out of the shop! Oh, my lungs, get out of the shop! Oh, my eyes and limbs—gorooo! Don't ask for money; make it an exchange."

I never was so frightened in my life, before or since; but I told him humbly that I wanted money, and that nothing else was of any use to me, but that I would wait for it, as he desired, outside, and had no wish to hurry him. So I went outside, and sat down in the shade in a corner. And I sat there so many hours, that the shade became sunlight, and the sunlight became shade again, and still I sat there waiting for my money. . . .

He made many attempts to induce me to submit to an exchange: at one time coming out with a fishing-rod, at another with a fiddle, at another with a cocked hat, at another with a flute. But I resisted all these overtures, and sat there in desperation; each time asking him with tears in my eyes for my money or my jacket. At last he began to pay me in halfpence at a time; and was full two hours getting by easy stages to a shilling.

"Oh, my eyes and limbs!" he then cried, peeping hideously out of the shop, after a long pause, "will you go for twopence more?"

"I can't," I said; "I shall be starved."

"Oh, my lungs and liver, will you go for threepence?"

"I would go for nothing, if I could," I said, "but I want the money badly."

"Oh, go-roo!" (It is really impossible to express how he twisted this ejaculation out of himself, as he peeped around the doorpost at me, showing nothing but his crafty old head.) "Will you go for fourpence?"

I was so faint and weary that I closed with this offer; and taking the money out of his claw, not without trembling, went away more hungry and thirsty than I had ever been, a little before sunset.

Exploration Points

1. How many unique mannerisms does this shopkeeper have?

    Every movement of this shopkeeper is extreme. He doesn't walk; he rushes. He doesn't greet; he seizes by the hair of the head. He grins rather than smiles and whines in a strange tune rather than talks. His speech is far too excited for the circumstance, and what's more, he repeats the crazy things he says as if to outdo his manic self. He rattles a strange sound in his throat—"Goroo!" Sometimes his eyes bug out of his head as he does so. Nervous energy flows into his hands, making them tremble.

    Dickens has done a great job of making me feel David Copperfield's intimidation. I certainly wouldn't want to find myself at the mercy of this strange man.

2. How has Dickens's description added to these wild mannerisms?

    A writer less facile than Dickens may not be able to create a believable character with this many eccentricities. To achieve believability, Dickens has used description of the shop's surroundings in some unique ways.

    The entire shop appears haphazard and chaotic, a reflection of the keeper's appearance and actions. The room is cramped, and the space is stuffed with hanging clothes. In the very first sentence, instead of saying a window is dirty, Dickens describes it as darkening rather than lighting the room. His choice of words sets up the unpredictability that David Copperfield will face in meeting the owner of this place. Dickens carries the window description further by noting that a second one displays not a pretty garden, but weeds that badly prick and a crippled donkey. As a result, we're not surprised to see that the shopkeeper is ugly, unshaven, dirty, and smelling of alcohol. And we're poised to more easily believe the man's crazed mannerisms of speech, bugging eyes, rattling throat, and trembling hands.

3. From what inner value(s) do you think these mannerisms spring?

According to E. M. Forster's definition of flat and round characters, this shopkeeper is flat. He may have many mannerisms, but he's constructed around a single idea or inner value, and he doesn't change. Every mannerism Dickens has attributed to him leads back to this man's inner value: making a fast, hard buck is all that matters. At first it appears that this man is stupid; he allows himself and his shop to appear so frightful that customers immediately want to leave. But toward the end of the scene, we see the man's cunning. I get the feeling that his appearance and wild actions are quite purposeful. They're all designed to give him the upper hand in transactions. If he'd immediately and quietly declared to his young customer that he would only make an exchange for the jacket or pay hardly anything, perhaps David Copperfield would have left in a hurry. Instead, the shopkeeper leads David on, all the while displaying his wildness, until the boy is frightened into practically giving the jacket away.

FROM

Compelling Evidence
by Steve Martini

Setting: present day. Attorney Paul Madriani waits in a bar to meet his ex-boss and mentor, Ben Potter. This is our introduction to Potter.

Then I see him moving from a table in the dining room toward the bar. Ben Potter. Tall, well over six feet, though I doubt he's ever been accurately measured. He has one of those frames, the shoulders rounded and hunched forward a little, the gait just slightly lumbering. He wears his usual dark vested sweater under his suit coat. Together with his bearing, this wrinkled bulk projects the image of some mighty bear aimlessly foraging for meat tied in a tree. He has managed to exploit this awkward posture, coin it as his own, so that a generation of law students who have studied under him in the evenings at the university now mimic this style when addressing juries. It's an attitude that on Ben is not tired or aging, but stately, deliberative.

Exploration Points

1. How does this character's choice of clothing work with his mannerisms to create a visual picture?

   Martini uses only two sentences to describe Ben Potter's clothing, yet they add much to his character. The "dark" and "wrinkled bulk" of layered clothing adds to the sense of corpulence, helping us envision a large bear. The word "usual" is well used. Within its own sentence, it merely tells us that Ben Potter always dresses this way without implying why. But paired with the phrase, "He has managed to exploit this awkward posture," the word "usual" takes on a whole new meaning, allowing us to see the deliberateness of Ben Potter's choice of clothing and actions.

2. What possible inner value might lead this character to "exploit [his] awkward posture"?

   Martini adds another interesting phrase to help us quickly envision Ben Potter: "so that a generation of law students who have studied under him in the evenings at the university now mimic this style when addressing juries." Suddenly we see Ben Potter not as some aging man who doesn't care to dress well or stand up straight, but as a teacher who is so authoritative, so impressive, that his students have taken his awkward mannerisms out of the classroom and into the courtroom, mimicking them while defending or prosecuting cases. This leads me to think, based solely on this passage, that Potter's corresponding inner value is a deep love and respect for the justice system. As a result of this inner value, he employs everything he can, including his unusual stance and gait, to impress upon his students the importance of learning every bit of information he presents.

Moving On

So now what?

After going through the personalizing process, you're beginning to understand your characters pretty well. Knowing your characters is important, but it's not an end in itself. Their inner values will play a big part in building your story. To see how your characters' unique inner values can create action and conflict within your novel, we turn to Secret #2: Action Objectives.

Action Objectives

ACTOR'S TECHNIQUE:

Through study of a role, an actor must determine the character's *objective*—the thing he strives for—both throughout the play as a whole and in each scene. The objective must be stated in terms of a specific *action*, that is, a verb, rather than a general state of being or a noun. (For example, within a scene: "I want to hurry my roommate out the door so I can have some time to myself" rather than "I want to be alone.") This *action objective* will guide the actor in creating appropriate movements needed to carry out that objective.

NOVELIST'S ADAPTATION

Before writing a scene, an author should first precisely determine the action objective of each character. In other words, what do the characters want to accomplish in the scene? These objectives should be specific to the situation and unique to the characters. Often, two characters' objectives will be at odds with each other. These objectives will provide clear motivation for the characters, giving rise to believable dialogue, action, and conflict.

In this chapter we turn from who a character *is* to what he or she *wants to accomplish*. Of course, these different facets can't be completely separated, for a character's inner values determine what the character wants, and vice versa. The truths you have discovered about your character(s) through personalizing will play an important role here. Through the use of action objectives you will learn how the unique aspects of your characters can help plot your novel.

In *An Actor Prepares*, Stanislavsky talks about breaking down a play into smaller units or "action objectives" that guide the actor on a course toward a character's overall "super-objective." This super-objective is the specific goal for which the character strives throughout the story as a whole. In other words, it's what the character Wants, with a capital W. Stanislavsky noted that any part of the play that did not relate to the super-objective would stand out as superfluous or wrong. Therefore, the better written the play, the stronger the pull of its super-objective.

The same principle is true for novels.

The Super-objective as the Character's Overall Desire

Before we examine our adaptation of action objectives for individual scenes, we first need to look at this concept of the super-objective, just as a contractor must review the plans for a house before beginning to stack bricks.

> The super-objective, or overall desire, of a character provides the foundation for action objectives in individual scenes.

The adaptation of this super-objective concept for novelists has led me to a character- and story-building process I call simply the Four Ds. An in-depth discussion of the Four Ds and how they apply to the main plot and all subplots within your novel could probably fill its own book and would take us more into the realm of story structure than characterization. Still, story affects characters and characters affect story; the two cannot help but overlap. For our purposes, we'll look at the Four Ds in terms of how they help define your main character and your central plot, focusing mainly on the first D. At the end of our discussion of each D, we'll look at an example from John Grisham's *The Firm*.

One thought before we move on. Some authors are careful pre-plotters. Others use a more free-form type of writing, starting with a character and discovering where that character takes them. If you're the latter type, don't despair at the plotting talk you're about to hear. The Four Ds can work equally as well for you as for all those pre-plotting types, because they allow you plenty of discovery room while providing just enough structure to ensure that you build a solid story. And for those of you who already have a plot in mind, the Four Ds provide an excellent tool for checking to see if your story builds to an effective climax without wandering.

The First D: Desire

Desire is the novelist's equivalent of Stanislavsky's super-objective.

Many times, authors build their stories based solely on conflict: "These are the problems my main character will face, and this is the outcome." But conflict implies opposition—an obstacle that stands in the way of something desired. In order for conflict to build scene by scene with the best logical and coherent progression, it must follow the course of a character's Desire, erecting larger and larger barriers for the character as the Desire is pursued. So before you begin the plotting—or writing—of every conflict in your novel, you should first ask your character: What is your innermost Desire that will propel you through this story?

Again, even though we will focus on a single main character as an example, remember that all of your main characters and important secondary characters should have a Desire. Conflicts between characters come into play when they are pursuing Desires that oppose one another.

Think of the Desire for your character in terms of your real-life friends. You know a friend not only by her appearance, her inner values, traits, and mannerisms; you also know her by her desires. One of the most important aspects of who she is lies in her deepest motivations. What does she *want* at this point in life? What does she strive for? This underlying motivation, or Desire, or super-objective, will drive her choices and actions.

In a novel, a character without a clear Desire can get lost in all the conflict, particularly if your story is action-filled. The result will be that regardless of how suspenseful the action, your readers simply won't connect with the characters well enough to care how they're affected by it.

Discovering your character's Desire is not always as simple as it may first appear. These two categories of knowledge will help guide you:

- the inner values that you discovered through personalizing
- the major problems in the story that the character will face

Admittedly, the second category presents something of a chicken-and-egg problem. The Desire helps lead you to the building of conflict within the story, yet you must know some of the major conflicts in order to determine Desire. The key word here is "major." You probably have in mind some of your story's main events. Using these main events to determine the character's Desire will lead you in building the smaller, individual units of conflict that link these events.

Your character's Desire may even partly arise from the inciting incident in your story—the first main event that sets into motion the novel's chain of conflict. For example, in a mystery the inciting incident may often be the murder. I say "partly" arise because the mere solving of the problem presented by the inciting incident sometimes is not specific enough to be the Desire in its entirety. Otherwise every detective novel would contain the very same Desire for the main character: to solve the crime. This is where the inner values of your character come into play. Using what you know of this detective—who he is *before* the crime takes place, personal issues in his life, and so on—will lead you to a Desire specific to him. The Desire could be something like: to earn a promotion through solving this difficult case; or, if for some reason he feels he could have prevented the crime: to ease his conscience by bringing the perpetrator of the crime to justice.

In discovering your character's Desire, note these three important points:

1. *The Desire must be stated in terms of an active verb.*

   A state-of-being verb doesn't work because it is so general in nature that it can't give rise to action. These would include such goals as "I want to be happy" or "I want to be loved." Let's say you determine your character's Desire will focus on having a happy marriage. So what must she do to achieve it? The answer will depend on her definition of a happy marriage. You'd have to ask your character to break down what a happy marriage means to her, then set her in pursuit of these goals. Her pursuit will naturally be stated in an active verb.

   As an example, in John Steinbeck's *The Pearl*, Kino and Juana live in poverty with their baby, Coyotito, in a little town near the ocean. When Kino finds a very valuable pearl—"the greatest pearl in the world"—his Desire arises. It is not merely a state-of-being Desire, as in "I want to be rich." Instead it is a Desire based on an active verb: to *sell* the pearl for its proper value so he can raise his family out of poverty.

2. *The Desire must be very specific.*

   Let's say your character says her main definition of a happy marriage is one of trust. The focus of her Desire will now be: to build trust within my marriage. Again, how does she do that? What does trust look like to her? Does it mean she must build so strong a belief in her husband's honesty that she no longer wonders if he's with another woman when he works late? Or does it mean her husband must commit to working shorter hours so she'll have no reason to worry? Or does it mean she must persuade him that *she's* trustworthy?

Again looking at *The Pearl*, note how specific is Kino's Desire. He doesn't want to just sell the pearl for some fast money. He wants to sell it at its full value. And his Desire doesn't stop there. As often happens, the Desire contains more than one part. The goal of his selling the pearl is to raise his family from poverty. Kino dreams of providing his son with an education, a luxury that Kino himself had never enjoyed.

3. *The Desire must be exactly correct for the character and story.*

The slightest mistake of intent may not seem like much when you pinpoint your character's Desire, but it will lead to a very different story in the end, just as two angled lines begin together, then grow farther and farther apart. Say you now discover that your character's specific Desire is: to build trust within my marriage by never again lying to my husband. Notice the two different parts. This Desire will lead your character to (1) take specific steps in overcoming her proclivity to lie *so that* (2) she can build trust within her marriage. The conflicts that arise in opposition to this Desire will take the form of various events about which she'll be tempted to lie. Her choices will be whether to give in to the temptation or remain true to her resolve to change. Now let's tweak that Desire just a little bit until it reads: to build trust within my marriage by never again being caught in a lie. Aha! What a difference the word "caught" makes! You can see the shift of the character's mindset as she pursues this Desire. She still wants trust in her marriage. At times this will mean she cannot lie for fear of being caught. But at other times it will mean she will lie with utmost manipulation and cunning.

When Steinbeck created Kino with his specific Desire, the author set Kino on an inevitable course that he will doggedly pursue even as one conflict after another arises. First Kino finds himself in danger because others want to steal the pearl. Then he loses his house and fishing boat. As his wife begins to tell him she thinks they should throw the pearl back into the sea because it is bringing them evil, Kino cannot listen. He remains obsessed with selling the pearl. Next, he finds that he can sell the pearl, but for far less than its real value, for would-be buyers want to cheat him. So he must set out on a journey with his wife and child to find the proper buyer. On the journey he places not only himself but also his wife and child in danger from those who would steal the pearl. Why does he not listen to his wife when she continues to say the pearl is bringing evil? Because of his very specific, two-part Desire, which propels him through the story Steinbeck wanted to write. The fact that part of Kino's Desire focuses on bettering his family sets up the irony of the story. His very obsession to richly provide for them by selling the pearl ends up taking from them what little they had—a house, their boat, and finally, Coyotito's life. Only then, with his family utterly ruined, does Kino abandon his Desire and throw the pearl back into the sea.

You may discover that your character has *two* main Desires—one conscious and the other subconscious. This tends to occur in more complex character-driven novels rather than in those driven by suspense, mystery, or action. The two Desires are often diametrically opposed to each other, causing internal conflict. The character will pursue the conscious Desire, thinking that this is the utmost goal. But the subconscious Desire will drive the character's actions in times of stress and decision-making. As events in the story unfold, the subconscious Desire will rise to the surface. The character will then begin to see this Desire and the inner value from which it springs. Many times at the end of such stories, the character must choose between the (originally) subconscious and conscious Desires, and will decide upon the former, realizing that it, indeed, was the driving force all along. If your character has both a conscious and an unconscious Desire, you will have to determine which of them is the ultimate driving force.

In *Gone With the Wind*, Scarlett O'Hara's conscious Desire is: to claim Ashley Wilkes as hers and hers alone. Through the entire long book, Scarlett lives through one conflict after another, always dreaming of Ashley, thinking she loves Ashley. But Scarlett's sub-conscious Desire is: to claim the love of a man who can make her—with all of her breathless, almost childlike passion for life—feel secure. At the end of the book, when Ashley's wife has died, leaving him finally free, Scarlett realizes that she never really loved him, for he was weaker than she. The man she really loves is Rhett Butler, her husband, the man who "comforted her when she woke in the nights crying with fright from her dreams." When Rhett leaves her, Scarlett doesn't revel in her sudden freedom to be with Ashley. Instead, all she can think of is winning back Rhett's love.

Example of Desire (from **The Firm** *by* **John Grisham)**

When young Mitch McDeere is wined and dined by the law firm of Bendini, Lambert & Locke before he even passes the bar, he's ecstatic over his good fortune. He'd had his sights set on a Wall Street firm, but this one offers him an incredible starting salary and bonus package complete with a new BMW in the color of his choice. He can make partner in about ten years, they tell him. The senior partners also inform Mitch he'll have to work ninety-hour weeks, but he doesn't care. All he can think of is the rich lifestyle that this firm promises for himself and his wife, Abby. He forgets his ideas of a Wall Street firm and accepts the offer. Mitch's Desire: to make partner at the firm so he and Abby can live the good life.

One final note about this first D. When you establish your character's Desire, you place within the reader's mind the inevitable question: Will he obtain it? The resolving of this question is your novel's "answering end." Your character will obtain his Desire or he won't. Or he may obtain it at far greater cost than he ever expected to pay. Or he may have the Desire within his grasp but decide he doesn't want it after all, as does Scarlett O'Hara. The possibilities are many.

Once you determine your character's Desire and the answering end of your story, you have a clear picture of your character's starting and finishing points. If you were to diagram your story, and your character obtains his Desire, it might look like this:

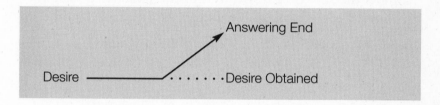

Desire ⟶ Desire Obtained (Answering End)

If the character does not obtain his Desire, the diagram might look like this:

Answering End

Desire ⟶ ·······Desire Obtained

The Second D: Distancing

The trouble with the first diagram above is that it represents a very boring novel. There's no satisfying story in a character's desiring something and homing in on a straight, unobstructed course to obtain it. Story occurs when a character meets opposition along the course of pursuing his Desire and then struggles to overcome it. The second D—Distancing—refers to the conflicts that arise as barriers to oppose your character as he pursues his Desire. These will form the main body of your novel. As these conflicts build upon one another, they push or "distance" your character farther and farther away from what he wants. This Distancing builds until your character reaches the third D.

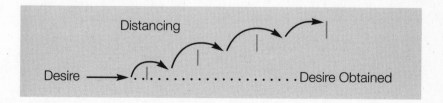

Distancing

Desire ⟶ ·.·.··················Desire Obtained

Example of Distancing (from The Firm *by John Grisham)*

Mitch works night and day, rarely seeing Abby, and their marriage begins to suffer. Then he hears that five partners from the firm have met bizarre accidental deaths. And things begin to seem strange within the walls of the firm. The fourth floor is strictly off limits, with no reason given. Mitch begins to feel as if he's not being told the truth about certain things. He decides to quietly investigate the partners' deaths. Then an FBI agent begins trailing him, dropping hints that the firm is involved in illegal activity. When Mitch reports this to the firm's partners, they tell him the FBI has been harassing them for years. Mitch doesn't know whom to believe.

The Third D: Denial

The third D is the Denial of your character's Desire. All the conflicts within the Distancing have risen to such a degree that it appears your character simply cannot attain his Desire, no matter how hard he has tried. In plot-driven novels the Denial may occur within a single scene. In character-driven stories, the Denial may be more subtle, spreading over numerous scenes as the character seems to hit a brick wall and perhaps even considers giving up his pursuit of the Desire.

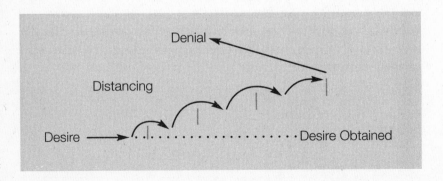

Example of Denial (from **The Firm** *by John Grisham)*

The FBI agent finally tells Mitch the whole story. Bendini, Lambert & Locke is a front for the Mafia, and the FBI is closing in on it. Mitch must cooperate with the FBI, passing agents inside information about the firm's illegal activities, or he will be indicted with everyone else when the FBI gathers its evidence. Mitch's dream of becoming partner and making millions with the firm is now completely unobtainable. If only he'd gone to Wall Street as he'd planned.

At this point, in stories with happy endings, the character often manages to turn things around, pushing aside all those Distancing conflicts and getting back on track to obtain his Desire. However, the most exciting plots add a final zinger before the character manages to overcome the opposition.

The Fourth D: Devastation

The Devastation suddenly twists the fate of the character from mere Denial of his Desire (as if that weren't bad enough) to an outcome so terrible that he hadn't even imagined its occurring. It serves as a final "gotcha" for the readers—just when they think things couldn't possibly get worse, they do.

As exciting as a Devastation can be, some stories simply can't include them because of certain constraints. A novella, for example, lacks the word length often needed for this final twist. Or a "sweet" romance may not want to take the conflict this far.

When a character meets a Devastation, he's often worse off than when the story began. In order to obtain his Desire now, he'll have to work harder than he ever imagined. Again, you'll need to know where the answering end of your story lies (at the point of Desire obtained, or somewhere else) so you can plot the course to it from the Devastation.

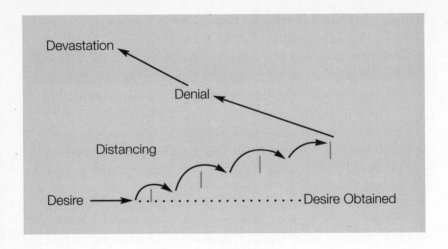

Example of Devastation (from* The Firm by *John Grisham)

An FBI agent turns traitor and sells the Mafia information about how Mitch is cooperating with the FBI. As a result, the Mafia wants to kill Mitch before he can deliver the bulk of the incriminating evidence to the government. But Mitch can no longer trust the FBI to protect him. He has no recourse but to go into hiding with his wife. Now, as a result of Mitch's greed, they are being hunted by both the Mafia and the FBI, and he will never be able to practice law again.

Using the Four Ds

Once you've determined the Four Ds of your novel (or perhaps Three Ds, if you don't include a Devastation), you'll know your story's key events, and creating individual scenes from one D to the next will be far easier. Your character will have a clear super-objective or Desire that pulls him through the story toward its answering end. Each scene, then, will be a small step as he pursues that Desire and meets opposition that pushes him off course.

If you're one of those free-form authors who doesn't like advance plotting, I encourage you not to write off the Four-D process without trying it. Free-form writing must follow *some* general parameters or the story will tend to wander. The most important thing will be to discover your character's Desire. Once you know a character's Desire, you'll be better positioned to allow that character to take you into unknown territory, for you'll have a clear sense of the character's innermost motivation. Without a strong Desire, what will determine your character's next steps? Try discovering the Four Ds as a basic outline, then allow your free-form methods to work as individual scenes unfold. There is still much room for last-minute creativity, for the possible paths that lead from one D to the next are infinite.

Action Objectives for Individual Scenes

Once you understand the process of the Four Ds, particularly the first—determining your character's super-objective or Desire—you can use its miniversion in writing scenes. The same basic principle applies: you must know what your character wants to accomplish. Just as your character approaches the novel in its entirety with a Desire, so she will approach each scene with an initial action objective—what she desires to accomplish in that scene. As the scene unfolds, conflicts will occur that make her obtaining of that desire difficult. These conflicts may come from other characters, whose own initial action objectives for the scene are at odds with hers. Or they may come from within herself or from nature. A new, smaller action objective will then arise within her as she seeks to overcome each conflict. In turn, each of these smaller objectives will prompt her to make a specific response in order to stay on the course of obtaining the initial action objective.

> Action objectives set the course for conflict, dialogue, and choices within a scene.

As the term implies, action objectives must be stated in the form of active rather than state-of-being verbs, for the same reasons that a character's Desire must be. However, as Stanislavsky notes, it's important to remember that *action* does not necessarily imply *activity*. An action objective can range from purely mechanical in nature—"to climb over this fence without hurting myself"—to purely psychological—"to make a decision between the two opportunities that beckon me."

In the same way that a character's overall Desire sets in place the answering end to your novel, so does your character's initial action objective for a scene set up the scene's answering end. At the scene's conclusion, your character will either achieve her initial action objective, draw closer to it, or be pushed farther from it.

Sometimes a scene will be so powerful that it will contain a miniversion of all Four Ds. In other words, the character will approach the scene with his action objective, the series of Distancing conflicts will lead him to a Denial, and then things will turn even worse—a Devastation. Scenes this strong are often turning points in a novel. We'll see an example of such a scene in the Study Samples at the end of this chapter.

To understand how action objectives work, let's look at the opening scene between Mr. Lockwood and Mr. Heathcliff in Emily Brontë's *Wuthering Heights*, which takes place in 1801. We'll take the scene step by step, noting how the action objectives of Lockwood change as conflict arises, and how those objectives prompt him to specific responses.

Lockwood's initial action objective for the scene is: to place himself within the good graces of his new landlord so he can remain in his rented home. Without being told the details that lead to this action objective, we are led to believe that Lockwood must have had good reason to think he'd angered the landlord. We come to understand this as we see the enduring strength of the action objective in light of all that occurs.

[Mr. Heathcliff] little imagined how my heart warmed toward him when I beheld his black eyes withdraw so suspiciously under their brows, as I rode up, and when his fingers sheltered themselves, with a jealous resolution, still further in his waistcoat, as I announced my name.

"Mr. Heathcliff!" I said.

A nod was the answer.

"Mr. Lockwood, your new tenant, sir. I do myself the honor of calling as soon as possible after my arrival, to express the hope that I have not inconvenienced you by my perseverance in soliciting the occupation of Thrushcross Grange: I heard yesterday you had had some thoughts—"

"Thrushcross Grange is my own, sir," he interrupted, wincing. "I should not allow anyone to inconvenience me, if I could hinder it—walk in!"

Because of his host's obvious displeasure at his visit, Lockwood's action objective now becomes: to enter the house without displeasing his landlord further. Response: He quickly accepts the grudging invitation, choosing to think of Heathcliff's demeanor as merely "reserved" and choosing not to take the surliness of Heathcliff's servant personally.

The "walk in" was uttered with closed teeth, and expressed the sentiment, "Go to the deuce": even the gate over which he leaned manifested no sympathizing movement to the words; and I think that circumstance determined me to accept the invitation: I felt interested in a man who seemed more exaggeratedly reserved than myself.

When he saw my horse's breast fairly pushing the barrier, he did put out his hand to unchain it, and then suddenly preceded me up the causeway, calling, as we entered the court—"Joseph, take Mr. Lockwood's horse; and bring up some wine."

Joseph was an elderly, nay an old man: very old, perhaps, though hale and sinewy. "The Lord help us!" he soliloquized in an undertone of peevish displeasure, while relieving me of my horse: looking, meantime, in my face so sourly that I charitably conjectured he must have need of divine aid to digest his dinner, and his pious ejaculation had no reference to my unexpected advent. . . .

Before passing the threshold, I paused to admire a quantity of grotesque carving lavished over the front, and especially about the principal door; above which, among a wilderness of crumbling griffins and shameless little boys, I detected the date "1500," and the name "Hareton Earnshaw."

One step brought us into the family sitting room, without any introductory lobby or passage . . . : they call it here "the house" preeminently. It includes kitchen and parlor, generally; but I believe at Wuthering Heights the kitchen is forced to retreat altogether into another quarter. . . . In an arch under a dresser reposed a huge, liver-colored bitch pointer, surrounded by a swarm of squealing puppies; and other dogs haunted other recesses. . . .

Mr. Heathcliff forms a singular contrast to his abode and style of living. He is a dark-skinned gypsy in aspect, in dress and manners a gentleman: that is, as much a gentleman as many a country squire: rather slovenly, perhaps, yet not looking amiss with his negligence, because he has an erect and handsome figure; and rather morose. Possibly, some people might suspect him of a degree of underbred pride; I have a sympathetic chord within that tells me it is nothing of the sort: I know, by instinct, his reserve springs from an aversion to showy displays of feeling—to manifestations of mutual kindliness. He'll love and hate equally under cover, and esteem it a species of impertinence to be loved or hated again.

As they seat themselves and Heathcliff fails to make conversation, Lockwood grows uncomfortable. His action objective then becomes: to find an action to fill the awkward silence. Response: He tries to pet the dog, even though it appears unfriendly.

I took a seat at the end of the hearthstone opposite that toward which my landlord advanced, and filled up an interval of silence by attempting to caress the canine mother, who had left her nursery, and was sneaking wolfishly to the back of my legs, her lip curled up, and her white teeth watering for a snatch. My caress provoked a long, guttural snarl.

"You'd better let the dog alone," growled Mr. Heathcliff in unison, checking fiercer demonstrations with the punch of his foot. "She's not accustomed to be spoiled—not kept for a pet." Then, striding to a side door, he shouted again, "Joseph!"

Joseph mumbled indistinctly in the depths of the cellar, but gave no intimation of ascending; so his master dived down to him, leaving me vis-à-vis the ruffianly bitch and a pair of grim, shaggy sheep dogs, who shared with her a jealous guardianship over all my movements.

The dogs make Lockwood even more uncomfortable. His new action objective: to keep the dogs from attacking. Response: He sits very still.

Not anxious to come in contact with their fangs, I sat still; but, imagining they would scarcely understand tacit insults, I unfortunately indulged in winking and making faces at the trio, and some turn of my physiognomy so irritated madam, that she suddenly broke into a fury and leaped on my knees.

Uh-oh, now Lockwood's really in trouble. His action objective: to get away from the dog. Response: He throws her aside and jumps behind a table.

I flung her back, and hastened to interpose the table between us. This proceeding roused the whole hive: half-a-dozen four-footed fiends, of various sizes and ages, issued from hidden dens to the common center. I felt my heels and coatlaps peculiar subjects of assault.

Completely outnumbered now, Lockwood realizes he is helpless. His action objective: to save himself from a potentially fatal attack. Response: He calls for help.

> Parrying off the larger combatants as effectually as I could with the poker, I was constrained to demand, aloud, assistance from some of the household in reestablishing peace.
>
> Mr. Heathcliff and his man climbed the cellar steps with vexatious phlegm: I don't think they moved one second faster than usual, though the hearth was an absolute tempest of worrying and yelping. Happily, an inhabitant of the kitchen made more dispatch: a lusty dame, with tucked-up gown, bare arms, and fire-flushed cheeks, rushed into the midst of us flourishing a frying pan: and used that weapon and her tongue, to such purpose, that the storm subsided magically, and she only remained, heaving like a sea after a high wind, when her master entered on the scene.
>
> "What the devil is the matter?" he asked, eyeing me in a manner that I could ill endure after this inhospitable treatment.

Lockwood's fear turns to anger, for the moment blotting out his initial action objective of wanting to please his host. His new objective: to defend his actions to Heathcliff. Response: He throws out accusations.

> "What the devil, indeed!" I muttered. "The herd of possessed swine could have had no worse spirits in them than those animals of yours, sir. You might as well leave a stranger with a brood of tigers!"
>
> "They won't meddle with persons who touch nothing," he remarked, putting the bottle before me, and restoring his displaced table. "The dogs do right to be vigilant. Take a glass of wine?"
>
> "No, thank you."

"Not bitten, are you?"

"If I had been, I would have set my signet on the biter."
Heathcliff's countenance relaxed into a grin.

"Come, come," he said, "you are flurried, Mr. Lockwood.
Here, take a little wine. Guests are so exceedingly rare in
this house that I and my dogs, I am willing to own, hardly
know how to receive them. Your health, sir!"

At Heathcliff's apology, Lockwood's anger quickly fades, and he
reconnects with the reason for his presence in the house. His new
action objective: to pull himself out of the mess he's made of the
visit. Response: He accepts the wine.

I bowed and returned the pledge; beginning to perceive
that it would be foolish to sit sulking for the misbehavior of
a pack of curs: besides, I felt loath to yield the fellow further
amusement at my expense, since the humor took that turn.

As you can see, Lockwood's initial action objective pulls him
through the entire scene. His reactions to the conflicts all reflect this
initial objective. Even when he lashes out at Heathcliff, his anger is
partly born of the disappointment that his strong objective of making a good impression has gone horribly awry.

This scene provides an example for an important point:

> As with overall Desire, a character's initial
> action objective for a scene must be exactly
> correct.

Take a look at Heathcliff. What would you say is his initial
action objective in this scene? He soon emerges as a complex person,
one who knows little of civility. However, even though he is ill-
disposed and ungracious toward his unexpected visitor, he does
invite Lockwood into his house, offer him wine, and even apologizes
when it's absolutely necessary to convince the man to stay. Focusing

on these basic choices, we could say his action objective is: to welcome his visitor. But if that is so, why all the conflict between the two men? Heathcliff's objective would seem to fit hand-in-glove with Lockwood's, and they should have a splendid visit. No, we must focus not only on Heathcliff's choices, but also on his demeanor, which is anything but welcoming. The author obviously had something far different in mind. I think Heathcliff's action objective is more along the lines of: to hide his incivility from this unexpected visitor. This action objective is similar in that it will involve playing host to the man. Yet it is entirely different in that it's not generous, focusing outwardly on Lockwood's needs. Instead it is purely self-gratifying and focused inward. Ironically, in this self-serving state, Heathcliff opens himself up to all his flaws of incivility, and they proceed to color all that he does. He fails quite miserably to obtain his initial action objective.

As you focus on action objectives to write your scenes, you'll see firsthand how effective they are in keeping your novel on course.

> The use of action objectives will guide every scene in your novel to move the story forward in a vital way.

Specifically, action objectives ensure that:

1. *No scene is superfluous.*

   If your character is following a set of action objectives that relate to his overall Desire, each scene will emerge as a logical step toward trying to attain that Desire, regardless of how far the Distancing conflicts have shoved him off course.

2. *Backstory can be added without stopping the action.*

   Strong action objectives strengthen a scene and allow it to carry extra weight. Between one action objective and the next, you can introduce bits (not page after page!) of backstory that help explain these current objectives, and readers will not feel as if the story is slowing. Rather, they will appreciate the backstory as a necessary part of the action objective itself.

3. *No scene is a mere setup for further events.*

   This is a follow-up to the point above. Once your novel is written, action objectives can provide a wonderful test to apply in editing your work. In each scene, can you see the character's initial action objective and subsequent.objectives? Or is your character doing little in the scene while you load it up with backstory? In other words, is the scene a logical progression toward your character's Desire or is it a mere shell in which you inform the reader of description, past experiences, and the like? If you cannot see clear action objectives that lead your character through the scene, cut it. Believe me; it will be boring.

4. *Your character's words and choices are true to her personalized identity and Desire.*

   With a clear set of action objectives to guide your character through each scene, she will appear believable and real. This is not to say that her emotions won't flow in different directions at times. Conflicting emotions are a part of human nature, and readers can identify. Sometimes an action a character takes will be ill-advised or downright wrong. But as we saw with Lockwood, these wrong choices will be the result of action objectives gone awry. The character wants something in particular, doesn't get it, and reacts in a negative way.

As we close this chapter, remember that the key to determining action objectives lies first in discovering your character's Desire, or super-objective, that will propel her through the story. Once you have personalized your character and understand her Desire, you are well on your way to building a coherent and compelling novel.

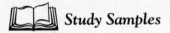 *Study Samples*

FROM

The Count of Monte Cristo
by Alexandre Dumas

Setting: France, early 1800s. In this scene, seventeen-year-old Mercedes speaks with her cousin, Fernand, who is wildly in love with her. Mercedes's initial action objective for the scene: to convince Fernand to stop asking her to marry him, for her heart belongs to Edmond Dantes. Fernand's initial action objective: to convince Mercedes to marry him.

"You see, Mercedes," said the young man, "here is Easter come round again; tell me, is this the moment for a wedding?"

"I have answered you a hundred times, Fernand, and really you must be very stupid to ask me again."

"Well, repeat it,—repeat it, I beg of you, that I may at last believe it! Tell me for the hundredth time that you refuse my love, which had your mother's sanction. Make me understand once for all that you are trifling with my happiness, that my life or death are nothing to you. Ah, to have dreamed for ten years of being your husband, Mercedes, and to lose that hope, which was the only stay of my existence!"

"At least it was not I who ever encouraged you in that hope, Fernand," replied Mercedes; "you cannot reproach me with the slightest coquetry. I have always said to you, 'I love you as a brother; but do not ask from me more than sisterly affection, for my heart is another's.' Is not this true, Fernand?"

"Yes, that is very true, Mercedes," replied the young man, "yes, you have been cruelly frank with me; but do you forget that it is among the Catalans a sacred law to intermarry?"

"You mistake, Fernand; it is not a law, but merely a custom, and, I pray of you, do not cite this custom in your favor. You are included in the conscription, Fernand, and are only at liberty on sufferance, liable at any moment to be called upon to take up arms. Once a soldier, what would you do with me, a poor orphan, forlorn, without fortune, with nothing but a half-ruined hut and a few ragged nets, the miserable inheritance left by my father to my mother, and by my mother to me? She has been dead a year, and you know, Fernand, I have subsisted almost entirely on public charity. Sometimes you pretend I am useful to you, and that is an excuse to share with me the produce of your fishing, and I accept it, Fernand, because you are the son of my father's brother, because we were brought up together, and still more because it would give you so much pain if I refuse. But I feel very deeply that this fish which I go and sell, and with the produce of which I buy the flax I spin,—I feel very keenly, Fernand, that this is charity."

"And if it were, Mercedes, poor and lone as you are, you suit me as well as the daughter of the first shipowner or the richest banker of Marseilles! What do such as we desire but a good wife and careful housekeeper, and where can I look for these better than in you?"

"Fernand," answered Mercedes, shaking her head, "a woman becomes a bad manager, and who shall say she will remain an honest woman, when she loves another man better than her husband? Rest content with my friendship, for I say once more that is all I can promise, and I will promise no more than I can bestow."

"I understand," replied Fernand, "you can endure your own wretchedness patiently, but you are afraid to share mine. Well, Mercedes, beloved by you, I would tempt fortune; you would bring me good luck, and I should become rich. I could extend my occupation as a fisherman, might get a place as clerk in a warehouse, and become in time a dealer myself."

"You could do no such thing, Fernand; you are a soldier, and if you remain at the Catalans it is because there is no war; so remain a fisherman, and contented with my friendship, as I cannot give you more."

"Well, I will do better, Mercedes. I will be a sailor; instead of the costume of our fathers, which you despise, I will wear a varnished hat, a striped shirt, and a blue jacket, with an anchor on the buttons. Would not that dress please you?"

"What do you mean?" asked Mercedes, with an angry glance,—"what do you mean? I do not understand you?"

"I mean, Mercedes, that you are thus harsh and cruel with me, because you are expecting some one who is thus attired; but perhaps he whom you await is inconstant, or if he is not, the sea is so to him."

"Fernand," cried Mercedes, "I believed you were good-hearted, and I was mistaken! Fernand, you are wicked to call to your aid jealousy and the anger of God! Yes, I will not deny it, I do await, and I do love him of whom you speak; and, if he does not return, instead of accusing him of the inconstancy which you insinuate, I will tell you that he died loving me and me only." The young girl made a gesture of rage. "I understand you, Fernand; you would be revenged on him because I do not love you; you would cross your Catalan knife with his dirk. What end would that answer? To lose you my friendship if he were conquered, and see that friendship changed into hate if you were victor. Believe me, to seek a quarrel with a man is a bad method of pleasing the woman who loves that man. No, Fernand, you will not thus give way to evil thoughts. Unable to have me for your wife, you will content yourself with having me for your friend and sister; and besides," she added, her eyes troubled and moistened with tears, "wait, wait, Fernand; you said just now that the sea was treacherous, and he has been gone four months, and during these four months there have been some terrible storms."

Fernand made no reply, nor did he attempt to check the tears which flowed down the cheeks of Mercedes, although for each of these tears he would have shed his heart's blood; but these tears flowed for another. He arose, paced a while up and down the hut, and then, suddenly stopping before Mercedes, with his eyes glowing and his hands clinched,— "Say, Mercedes," he said, "once for all, is this your final determination?"

"I love Edmond Dantes," the young girl calmly replied, "and none but Edmond shall ever be my husband."

"And you will always love him?"

"As long as I live."

Fernand let fall his head like a defeated man, heaved a sigh that was like a groan, and then suddenly looking her full in the face, with clinched teeth and expanded nostrils, said,—"But if he is dead"—

"If he is dead, I shall die too."

"If he has forgotten you"—

"Mercedes!" called a joyous voice from without,—"Mercedes!"

"Ah," exclaimed the young girl, blushing with delight, and fairly leaping in excess of love, "you see he has not forgotten me, for here he is!" And rushing towards the door, she opened it, saying, "Here, Edmond, here I am!"

Fernand, pale and trembling, drew back, like a traveller at the sight of a serpent, and fell into a chair beside him. Edmond and Mercedes were clasped in each other's arms. The burning Marseilles sun, which shot into the room through the open door, covered them with a flood of light. At first they saw nothing round them. Their intense happiness isolated them from all the rest of the world, and they only spoke in broken words, which are the tokens of a joy so extreme that they seem rather the expression of sorrow. Suddenly Edmond saw the gloomy, pale, and threatening countenance of Fernand, as it was defined in the shadow. By a movement for which he could scarcely account to himself, the young Catalan placed his hand on the knife at his belt.

"Ah, your pardon," said Dantes, frowning in his turn; "I did not perceive that there were three of us." Then, turning to Mercedes, he inquired, "Who is this gentleman?"

"One who will be your best friend, Dantes, for he is my friend, my cousin, my brother; it is Fernand—the man whom, after you, Edmond, I love the best in the world. Do you not remember him?"

"Yes!" said Dantes, and without relinquishing Mercedes' hand clasped in one of his own, he extended the other to the Catalan with a cordial air. But Fernand, instead of responding to this amiable gesture, remained mute and trembling. Edmond then cast his eyes scrutinizingly at the agitated and embarrassed Mercedes, and then again on the gloomy and menacing Fernand. This look told him all, and his anger waxed hot.

"I did not know, when I came with such haste to you, that I was to meet an enemy here."

"An enemy!" cried Mercedes, with an angry look at her cousin. "An enemy in my house, do you say, Edmond! If I believed that, I would place my arm under yours and go with you to Marseilles, leaving the house to return to it no more." Fernand's eye darted lightning. "And should any misfortune occur to you, dear Edmond," she continued with the same calmness which proved to Fernand that the young girl had read the very innermost depths of his sinister thought, "if misfortune should occur to you, I would ascend the highest point of the Cape de Morgion and cast myself headlong from it."

Fernand became deadly pale. "But you are deceived, Edmond," she continued. "You have no enemy here—there is no one but Fernand, my brother, who will grasp your hand as a devoted friend."

And at these words the young girl fixed her imperious look on the Catalan, who, as if fascinated by it, came slowly towards Edmond, and offered him his hand. His hatred, like a powerless though furious wave, was broken against the strong ascendancy which Mercedes exercised over him. Scarcely, however, had he touched Edmond's hand than he felt he had done all he could do, and rushed hastily out of the house.

Exploration Points

1. How do Mercedes's and Fernand's initial action objectives prompt their responses throughout the scene?

   Mercedes approaches this scene with a very strong action objective. She will not be swayed in convincing Fernand that she loves another. Apparently, from her demeanor, she has had to deal with his persistence many times, and has grown tired of it. Unfortunately for her, Fernand's action objective is just as strong.

   First Fernand brings up the subject of a wedding. Mercedes's action objective immediately becomes: to cut this conversation short. Response: She calls him stupid for even asking again. Fernand amends his action objective slightly so that it becomes: to use various forms of argument to change Mercedes's mind. He tries guilt, saying that Mercedes's mother approved of their marriage and that Mercedes is making him miserable by refusing him. Mercedes refuses the guilt. Then Fernand alleges that she is disobeying a sacred law by not marrying him. Mercedes says it is not a law but merely a custom. Then she turns the tables on him, saying in effect that *he* is bound by the law, for he is a soldier and could be called to battle any moment. Then, if she were his wife, what would become of her? She is too poor to be of financial help to him. Fernand responds that her poverty doesn't matter to him. Here, Mercedes reminds him of her ultimate reason—she loves another man. Fernand tries guilt once more— "instead of the costume of our fathers, which you despise, I will wear a varnished hat . . ."

Fernand's action objective now becomes: to persuade Mercedes that Edmond will not return to her, because of either inconstancy or death at sea. Mercedes new action objective: to defend Edmond. When Fernand asks her "final determination," she declares her ultimate response—"None but Edmond shall ever be my husband." Fernand challenges her. What if Edmond is indeed dead or has forgotten her?

When Edmond Dantes unexpectedly appears and asks who Fernand is, Mercedes's action objective is twofold: to set Edmond's mind at rest by declaring her love for him and to pave the way for him and Fernand to be friends. Fernand's action objective: to hold himself together in the sudden presence of his enemy. Unfortunately for Fernand, he cannot bring himself to be cordial, and his mere countenance makes Edmond realize he is an enemy. Mercedes's action objective: to prove to Edmond that her love for him is more important than her friendship love for Fernand—"If I believed that, I would place my arm under yours . . . leaving the house to return to it no more."

When Mercedes sees the pure hatred in Fernand's eyes, a new action objective arises: to protect Edmond. She declares that if misfortune occurred to Edmond, she would kill herself. Then she exerts her power over Fernand to make him take Edmond's hand in friendship. Fernand's action objective: to protect whatever relationship he still has with Mercedes. Response: he forces himself to take Edmond's hand.

2. From Fernand's point of view, this scene is so powerful that it works almost like a mininovel, incorporating all the Four Ds. If Fernand's initial action objective (to convince Mercedes to marry him) serves as the first D, his Desire, what are the other three?

The other three Ds lead the scene in logical progression from Fernand's Desire to the answering end.

Distancing: The series of conflicts leading to the Denial. Fernand can't persuade Mercedes to change her mind. She won't yield in the face of guilt or any of the other arguments Fernand presents. Then she becomes angry with him. She refuses to allow herself the smallest doubt that Edmond will return. When Fernand continues to imply that Edmond could be dead or untrustworthy, Mercedes goes even further, declaring that if Edmond were to die, she would die, too. In short, there is no way that Fernand can ever win her love, even with Edmond out of the picture.

Denial: Fernand sees Mercedes in the arms of his rival, again declaring her love for Edmond even to the point of killing herself if Edmond were to die.

Devastation: Not only has Fernand failed to win Mercedes for himself, but now in order to see her again even in friendship, he must extend his hand to the man he despises. The deed proves too much for him.

3. Look at a scene you have written and determine the characters' initial action objectives and subsequent objectives. Are they clear? Do the characters act and react with logical coherence? Do any of their actions seem out of sync with their overall Desire? Make any changes necessary to strengthen the scene, applying the Four Ds and action objectives as appropriate.

FROM
Black Lightning
by John Saul

Setting: present day. This scene is filled with psychological action objectives and serves as an example of how backstory can be interjected between them. The backstory here is particularly necessary since this scene gives readers their first direct look at Richard Kraven, the convicted serial killer. While waiting to view Kraven's execution, reporter Anne Jeffers is troubled by the thought that she helped send the man to his death through her series of articles that called for his conviction. She tells herself she should feel no remorse; Kraven is guilty, and besides, she was not on the jury that convicted him. Just before the execution,

Anne receives word that Kraven wants to see her. She agrees to meet with him one last time, wondering if, after all her interviews with him, he's finally going to confess. She is escorted to his cell.

Anne glanced at Kraven's hands for a moment, her eyes fixing on the long, strong fingers, the heavy tendons, and the thick veins starkly etched against Kraven's pale skin. An image rose in her mind of those hands sunk deep into the organs and entrails of his victims. Involuntarily, she took a step back.

Pulling her eyes away from Richard Kraven's hands, Anne forced herself to look directly into his face.

Though he was past forty, Kraven looked to be no more than thirty. The coal-black, wavy hair that had given his features a vaguely Byronic look had been shaved off the night before, but his face was exactly as Anne remembered it from his trial.

The softly curved, almost voluptuous lips; the straight, aquiline nose and wide-set eyes—movie star eyes, Anne had always called them—were the same as they had always been. No lines showed in his pale skin, no creases had formed around his eyes or mouth. When he spoke, it was as if he'd read her mind.

"If I were guilty, don't you think it would show in my face by now? Don't you think just the knowledge of what I'd done would have started to change me?"

Even his voice was the same, soft and reasonable.

"Did you ever hear of Dorian Gray?" Anne countered.

Kraven's lips tightened slightly, but the flatness in his eyes didn't change at all. It was that look that Anne remembered most, the cold flatness that had been the first thing she noticed about Kraven when she met him four years ago, after he'd been arrested in Bridgeport and it seemed as if every reporter in Seattle had gone to Connecticut on the same plane. It was those eyes that made his face a terrifying mask of almost alluring cruelty back then, and now, as he trained them fully on her, their effect hadn't changed.

"Shouldn't you be a bit more gracious?" he asked. "After all, you've finally convinced them to kill me."

Anne shook her head. "I wasn't on the jury, and I wasn't the judge. I wasn't even a witness. Neither at the trial nor to any of the things you did."

Richard Kraven offered Anne Jeffers the smile that had convinced so many people he was innocent. Had it not been for the flatness in his eyes, his expression would have looked almost wry. "Then how can you be so sure I did anything?"

"The evidence," Anne replied. Her eyes flicked toward the closed door at the end of the hall, and the guard, who was watching through a glass panel. How quickly could he open that door? Again it was as if Kraven could read her mind.

"Surely you don't think I'm any danger to you?" he asked, his voice taking on a warm concern that would have soothed Anne if it had come from anyone else.

How does he do it? Anne wondered. How does he make himself sound so normal? Except for the shaved head and the prison clothes, Richard Kraven still looked exactly like the popular young electronics professor he had once been, back when his star was still rising at the University of Washington. "I think if you had the chance, you would kill me right now," she said, keeping her voice level by sheer force of will. "I think if you weren't behind those bars, you would strangle me the way you did with all the others." As she stared into his expressionless eyes, Anne felt fury rising up in her. Why wouldn't he admit what he was, what he'd done? Her voice rose a notch. "How many were there, Kraven? Besides the three you were convicted of, how many? How many just in Seattle? Five? Seven?" There was still no reaction at all in Kraven's eyes, and Anne felt her rage building. There had to be some way to get through to this—this what? Man? But Richard Kraven wasn't a man. He was a monster.

A cold, unfeeling monster who had never acknowledged what he'd done, let alone shown any remorse. "Have we even found all the bodies yet?" she demanded. "For God's sake, Kraven, at least tell me that it's all finally going to be over!"

His flat gaze fixed steadily on her, but when Richard Kraven finally spoke, his voice again belied that strange dead look his eyes projected. "How can I tell you what I don't know?" he asked in a tone that reminded Anne of an earnest child.

Her jaw set as the heat of her anger suddenly turned ice cold. "Why did you want to see me?" she demanded. "What could you possibly have to say?"

Richard Kraven smiled again, but this time there was no warmth to his smile at all; the cold, unblinking eyes fixed on her, the jaw tightened, and in that hard, grim look Anne Jeffers was certain she was at last seeing the true face of the evil that dwelt within Richard Kraven. "Today won't end it. Killing me won't end it," he said, each word a chip of ice. "That's what I wanted to tell you, Anne. How will you feel, Anne? When I'm dead, and it all starts again, how will you feel?" . . .

Anne took a step backward, then turned and strode quickly down the corridor toward the exit.

Exploration Points

1. Anne Jeffers's initial action objective is: to hear Kraven's last words as final evidence that she did the right thing in calling for his death. What are her subsequent objectives as she reacts to Kraven throughout the scene?

   When Anne first sees Kraven she is reminded of his crimes, and before she can stop herself, she shows her fear by taking a step back from his cell. Immediately she is sorry that she did so. Her next objective is: to hide the fact that he intimidates and scares her even though he is behind bars. Response: she forces herself to look into Kraven's eyes.

Still playing the innocent, Kraven speaks in a reasonable voice that could be so convincing if Anne didn't know otherwise. Her next objective: to prove he cannot change her mind, because she knows he is a liar. Response: she compares him to Dorian Gray, a known liar from classic literature.

Kraven is not happy with the comparison. He tries another tactic—accusation—by implying that Anne is responsible for his execution. Here, Kraven's cunning is particularly apparent. He seems to know that this is a sore point. Anne has already spent time convincing herself she is not to blame, and so will not allow herself to be led down this path. Her objective: to cut this accusation short by presenting solid evidence that Kraven himself, not she, is responsible for the execution. Response: she shakes her head and states her arguments, then turns the blame back on Kraven himself, reminding him of the crimes he committed.

Kraven will not give up. He again tries to convince Anne he is innocent, using her own argument. Since she wasn't a witness to the crimes, how can she be so sure? Anne's objective: to stand her ground, even while Kraven is making her nervous. Response: she replies, "The evidence." But her eyes involuntarily flick toward the door, again betraying her fear.

Kraven changes tactics again, suggesting that Anne's fear is evidence that she isn't thinking straight. "Surely you don't think I'm any danger to you?" he asks, implying that if she is silly enough to be unsure of her safety even when he's behind bars, her other reasoning may be just as illogical. Anne is disgusted at Kraven's mask of normalcy. Her objective: to tell him she knows he is a monster bent on killing. Response: she says he would kill her if he could, then accuses him of committing many other murders for which he's never been held accountable. Her disgust mounts to anger. When Kraven again denies his culpability, Anne has had enough and demands to know why he wanted to see her.

Kraven now has Anne right where he wants her. He tells her that the murders will continue after he dies, and that she will be responsible. Anne realizes that Kraven will never confess. What's more, he continues to hit her sore spot. Objective: to get away from this detestable man. Response: she hurries away.

2. What is the answering end to this scene that is set up by Anne's initial action objective? Does she obtain it?

The answering end for Anne is whether or not she finally hears Kraven's confession to the crimes, which would prove to her that she has been right to call for his execution. Anne fails miserably to attain her initial action objective. Not only does Kraven tell her she's done the wrong thing, he goes so far as to say *she* will be responsible for future murders.

3. Read the scene again, noting the movement from one action objective to another and the interjected backstory. How does each bit of backstory relate to its action objective?

John Saul has cleverly woven backstory into this scene, telling us quite a bit about Kraven and his crimes without stopping the action. The first bit of backstory occurs in the second sentence, when Anne pictures Kraven's hands "sunk deep into the organs and entrails of his victims." This detail of a body-dismantling type of murder depicts the heinousness of Kraven's crimes and allows the reader to instantly understand Anne's fear as well as her disgust at his lack of remorse.

The next bit of backstory speaks of Kraven's arrest four years earlier in Connecticut. The immediate response of reporters in Seattle to the news conveys the high media coverage of the murders. Saul weaves in the fact that Kraven's eyes were as cold and flat then as they are now. This lack of change in Kraven's expression only adds to his hardness as he continually denies culpability for the crimes. And it heightens Anne's resolve to gain a confession from him.

We next hear of Kraven's background as an electronics professor. The fact that he looks as normal now as he did then helps spur Anne to anger. When she accuses him of committing even more murders than the three for which he was convicted (another piece of backstory) and demands to know why he wanted to see her, she pushes him to make the statement he's been leading toward all along—*she's* the guilty one.

Moving On

With personalizing and the determination of your character's Desire and action objectives in place, we look now to a technique dealing solely with dialogue. How can you make dialogue adequately reflect all that you now know of your character? The answer lies in Secret #3, Subtexting.

Subtexting

Without an inner reason for existence, lines in a play will be simply words, recited by rote, lacking believable emotion. When an actor looks beneath the lines to fully understand a character's desires and fears—the *subtext* of what is spoken—the words spring to life. As an actor interprets the subtext through such means as gestures and facial expression, the lines become layered with meaning, often far deeper than what is actually spoken. They express a character's strengths, weaknesses, passions. They bare a human soul.

NOVELIST'S ADAPTATION:

In realistic dialogue, characters will not always say what they mean. Communication often goes far deeper than words, flowing from the underlying meaning, or *subtext*. The key is to know when subtexted dialogue is appropriate, and how to convey the underlying meaning to readers.

Plays could not exist without subtexting. Most plays are the record of a particular truth trying to break through human action, and if every character merely spoke what was on his mind, dramatic tension couldn't be sustained for more than ten minutes. The truth of the play breaks forth a little here, a little there, until at the climax, at least in naturalistic theater, we see the moment of most intense honesty.

Subtexting is just as important in novels.

How many times have you read a novel with dialogue that struck you as shallow or unbelievable? Most of the time, this results from characters always saying exactly what they mean. I call this WYSIWYG dialogue—What You See Is What You Get. You may remember this term from the computer industry. First we had software that showed every command onscreen. Very confusing, with all those symbols. Then came the invention of WYSIWYG software, in which a bolded word is bold onscreen, an italicized word appears in italics. WYSIWYG may be fabulous in computers, but it's often faulty in conversation, because continuous use of this kind of dialogue does not reflect real life. As the Adaptation notes, people often communicate through subtexting, a meaning that has little to do with what's actually spoken.

An Introduction to Subtexting

Subtexting goes hand in hand with Secret #2, Action Objectives. When a character approaches a conversation with a clear objective that he does not want to reveal directly, a subtexted conversation is born.

Understanding the use of subtexting in dialogue is particularly difficult for inexperienced writers. Often a new novelist's tendency is to use WYSIWYG conversation because he has not yet grasped how to convey meaning without actually *saying* it. Since novels call for at least some dialogue in the majority of scenes, a lack of subtexting presents a major problem for a story. When a novelist learns how to employ subtexting effectively, dialogue that had once been lifeless and on-the-surface is transformed into vibrant interchanges between characters, pulling the reader into the story.

We all know that every piece of fiction, whether play or novel, short story or saga, is at heart a reflection of life's most basic struggles—love, fear, pain, defeat, and so on. Therefore, in order to write dialogue that is vibrant and realistic, that portrays these struggles convincingly, we first need to understand subtexting as it occurs in the real world. Here are a few important points:

- Subtexting is not limited to times when one is tongue-tied or tense. It's a common, everyday occurrence.
- Subtexting is not limited to conversations between people who have just met. It occurs in all relationships and is equally common between friends and enemies, strangers and spouses.
- Sometimes entire conversations are subtexted; other times only portions are.

Imagine two friends, Liz and Sara, working together on a volunteer project at church. Liz becomes irritated at something Sara does and snaps at her but soon apologizes. Sara is hurt and doesn't readily accept the apology. They say little while they continue to work. After their project is done, Liz suggests, "Want to go out for coffee? I'm buying." However, going out for coffee is a side issue. What she really means is: "Please, will you forgive me now? I'm truly sorry for what I said, and I want to prove it by treating you to coffee." (Action Objective: to prove she is sorry.) Sara will instinctively respond within the same subtext. If she says, "Okay, let's go" or even "I can't right now, but I'd love to later," what she would mean is: "Yes, I'm now ready to forgive you." (Action Objective: to convey she accepts the apology.) However, a chilled "I don't have time for that" would be a clear message that she still refuses to forgive.

What's fascinating here is that both women engage in this surface dialogue while knowing that the other isn't fooled one bit as to its underlying meaning. Their conversation is about coffee. But their *communication* is about forgiveness.

A Deeper Look at Subtexting

"Morning."

"Morning."

"Sleep well?"

"Yeah."

Five words spoken between man and wife. Sound mundane, boring? They are, in the form of WYSIWYG dialogue. But put your creativity to work; imagine the underlying messages these simple words could convey. Notice how your thoughts immediately shift from the words themselves to character motivation. Who are these people? What do they want? What kind of marriage do they have? What current conflicts do they face? Now you are thinking in a way that fleshes out your characters.

Just to show how effective subtexting can be, let's create a scene with maximum dichotomy between the dialogue and its subtext. Using only these five innocuous words, we'll depict a deeply flawed, abusive marriage. The conversation will be morning greetings; the communication will be about power and the need for love.

But wait a minute. If this subtext isn't in the dialogue itself, where will it be? How will we convey the real communication to the reader?

> In subtexting, the real communication is artfully woven through description into the context of the conversation.

The amount of description necessary will depend on how well readers know our characters. If our scene is in the middle of a novel and involves an ongoing conflict, the general context will already be in place, and less description is necessary. But let's raise the stakes in our example, making it the opening scene in a novel. Since readers will not know our characters at all, we'll need to skillfully weave adequate description into the scene—without stopping the action—in order to communicate the subtext.

At last, silence. Not even a creak from the padded rocking chair. She was too exhausted to push.

Early morning light filtered through checkered curtains, patterning the floor at Missy Danton's feet. Her newborn nursed in her arms, sighing in contentment with each swallow. For hours, Missy had despaired of this moment ever arriving. The baby had squalled all night, filling her with fear at the thought of waking her husband.

Missy smoothed a fingertip over the baby's perfect cheek. How could Franklin still treat her so badly after she'd given him such a beautiful son? She'd been so sure a baby would change things. But the pain in her left shoulder where he'd punched her twice yesterday, baby in her arms, screamed the bitter truth.

The nursery door pushed open. Missy raised dull eyes to watch Franklin's head appear, hair matted from sleep. What she would give for the slightest bit of compassion.

"Morning." Her voice was little more than a croak.

He slouched in the doorway, dismissive eyes flicking over her face, the baby. Languidly then, he stretched, yawning with exaggeration. "Morning."

Resentment rose like hot acid within Missy. She pressed her lips together, fingers tensing under the baby's blanket. "Sleep well?" Biting with sarcasm, the words slipped from her lips of their own accord. The moment they were out, she wanted them back.

Franklin drew to his full height, eyes narrowing. His head tilted, and Missy could see the telltale vein on his neck begin to throb. She braced herself, drawing her baby closer. Franklin's mouth opened in a smirk, his chin jutting. "Yeah," he challenged, goading, daring her to continue in such foolishness.

Fresh, nauseating fear blanketed Missy's anger. She now had more than herself to protect. Missy lowered her eyes.

Any doubt this woman's in real trouble? Afraid, seething with repressed anger, yearning for a gentle touch, caught in the web of victimization. And the baby. Notice how the son she'd "given" Franklin becomes "her baby" in the moment of danger. How long until this child is himself abused? We can be sure that Franklin does not intend to change his ways.

Yet none of this is spoken.

Let's take a look at the dialogue again, this time with its subtext:

"Morning."	*Look at me just once with compassion, Franklin. I've been up all night with the son I've given you, and I'm exhausted.*
"Morning."	*Yeah, what do I care? That's your place, watching the kid while I get my eight hours.*
"Sleep well?"	*I'm sick of the way you treat me! You make me furious! How can you be so selfish, sleeping all night while I was having so much trouble!*
"Yeah."	*You keep it up, Missy, you'll be sorry. A baby in your arms ain't gonna keep me from hitting you.*

The scene does contain one more line—an unspoken one. But the subtext is clear:

Missy lowered her eyes.	*I didn't mean it, Franklin, please don't hit me. I'm afraid for my baby.*

When to Subtext

How can you know when to subtext a scene? Not all dialogue should be subtexted; sometimes WYSIWYG exchanges are entirely appropriate. As with so many aspects of writing fiction, there are no cut-and-dried rules. But there are some major guidelines that, when considered together, can point you in the right direction, like beacons guiding a ship to port.

The key, as we've noted, is to write dialogue that's realistic. Therefore, *the first step in learning when to subtext a scene is to observe when subtexting occurs in real life.* Once you start listening for subtexting in conversations, including your own, you'll be amazed at how common it is. And the more familiar you become with this quirk of human nature, the better you'll be at re-creating it. When you notice subtexting within a conversation, ask yourself these questions:

- Why didn't the first person say exactly what she was thinking?
- Why didn't the second person?
- How was I able to understand the underlying meaning?
- If I were to write this scene, how would I convey its subtext?

The first two questions will teach you when to subtext in your writing. These questions will have one of two answers: (1) The person didn't *want* to state what she was thinking, or (2) The person didn't *need* to state what she was thinking, because the other person already knew it.

In our scene, Missy is an example of answer number one. She didn't want to say what she was thinking because she was afraid of her husband. Franklin, on the other hand, didn't need to say what he was thinking because he'd already spent months putting Missy "in her place." He could display his power all he wanted, whether through exaggerated yawn or foreboding stance, knowing she'd meekly accept it because of her fear.

> Guideline 1: One of these two reasons—not wanting or not needing to state what he's thinking—must apply to a character's motivation in order for subtexting to be considered in your dialogue.

With this first guideline in mind, ask yourself these questions regarding your scene:

- What does Character A want as a result of this conversation? Character B?
- Is A willing to state what's on her mind? Is B?
- Do A and B understand the current situation well enough that they don't need to state the obvious?
- Is this scene a continued presentation of an ongoing conflict, or is it a major turning point for change?

The first three questions consider character motivation. As we've noted, if a character doesn't want or doesn't need to state what he's thinking, subtexting may be appropriate. The fourth question considers the placement of the scene within your novel.

> Guideline 2: If the scene depicts an ongoing conflict, subtexting may be appropriate; however, a major turning point for change often demands honesty.

Think ahead in Franklin and Missy's story, after a series of events has caused Franklin to change. Imagine a critical scene in which the couple speaks openly for the first time. Missy is finally able to say what she feels, telling Franklin that after all his abuse, she doubts she can love him again even though he's now different. At this point, the conflict within Missy shifts from the struggle to survive as a battered wife to the struggle to regain lost love for her husband. Note here a wonderful by-product of effective subtexting. The bitter honesty you save for crucial scenes will be far more intense when such openness is new to the characters.

For scenes of ongoing conflict, keep in mind:

> Guideline 3: The older and/or deeper the conflict, the more likely that subtexting will be appropriate.

This doesn't mean that a small tiff can't be subtexted, as noted in the "coffee conversation" between Liz and Sara. It does mean that ancient, deep wounds between two people often are too painful or too tiring to speak of, though the residual effects of those wounds can seep into the subtext of everyday conversation.

How to Write Subtexted Dialogue

Before you write your own scene, study subtexting in other fiction. First, as we did with our scene, substitute the spoken words with their subtext. Then highlight all the descriptive words that conveyed this meaning to you. When you highlight these words, you'll notice that the description tends to fall into four major areas. These areas can most easily be remembered through the acronym TIME: Thought, Inflection, Movement, and Expression. Our scene between Missy and Franklin provides examples of each.

Thought   *How could Franklin still treat her with such contempt after she'd given him such a beautiful son? She'd been so sure a baby would change things. But the pain in her left shoulder where he'd punched her twice yesterday, baby in her arms, screamed the bitter truth.*

Inflection	*"Morning." Her voice was little more than a croak.*
Movement	*He slouched in the doorway, dismissive eyes flicking over her face, the baby.*
Expression	*Franklin's mouth opened in a smirk, his chin jutting.*

When you're ready to write your own subtexted dialogue, here are three steps to follow:

1. *Write out the subtext in your scene line by line.*

   This exercise will firmly establish in your own mind the underlying meaning of each spoken word. Subtext must be very clear to you before you can convey it to readers.

2. *Create overlying dialogue that would naturally occur in the scene.*

   Again, let's look at Missy and Franklin. That scene takes place not long after dawn. An exchange of morning greetings is a natural occurrence in that situation. In another example, if a woman is attracted to a man sitting beside her on the commuter train, she might initiate a conversation about the book he's reading. Their discussion of two characters in the story could parallel what they are thinking about each other and the impressions they want to create.

3. *Weave TIME description around the dialogue to convey the subtext.*
   A little more detail about each of these:

   - *Thought.* Note that this does not refer to italicized words that represent literal thoughts. These quickly become tiring to the reader and should be used sparingly. Rather, it denotes a clear indication of what a character is thinking through narrative. A word of caution here, since thought is often the easiest technique to employ. Don't overuse it, or you will simply move all meaning from spoken word to narrative. This will negate the need for other description and will deaden your scene, telling your story rather than showing it. One way to guard against overuse of thought is to stay within one point of view per scene. Note that in our example we remained in Missy's point of view yet always knew what Franklin was thinking, based on his actions and Missy's interpretations.

- *Inflection*. One or two well chosen words here can convey a magnitude of meaning. Missy's "Sleep well?" asked with biting sarcasm spoke of her deep resentment and anger at Franklin. It had nothing to do with how he'd spent his night.

- *Movement*. This incorporates body language as well as large motions. A slouch, a jiggling foot, a flick of the hand—all convey messages.

- *Expression*. Facial expression can be very effective even when a character is otherwise still. Remember that Missy's final communication of accepting "her place" under Franklin's abusive rule was conveyed merely through lowering her eyes. Such silent expression can tell the reader far more than words.

All these guidelines and steps may have you thinking, "Good grief, with all this to do in writing dialogue, I'll *never* finish my novel!" Truth is, you won't need to follow them for long. Once you become familiar with subtexting, it will become a natural process as you write. And you will see how much more depth and richness it lends to your scenes. Subtexting, by its very definition, will force you to create more description than you used when your characters always said exactly what they meant. Your dialogue will be more realistic and your characters more vibrant.

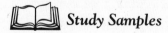 ## Study Samples

Here are excerpts from two scenes that use subtexted dialogue to varying degrees. Note how both incorporate dialogue natural to the scene while adding TIME description to convey the real communication. In the first scene, two "friends" speak politely and with affection while feeling something far different. In the second scene, a man and a woman struggle to rein in their attraction for each other.

FROM

Sense and Sensibility
by Jane Austen

Setting: England, early 1800s. In this novel, many scenes are subtexted as the characters squeeze their interior lives into the narrow constraints of social convention. Elinor Dashwood, a properly bred young lady, is in love with her sister-in-law's brother, Edward Ferrars, and believes that he loves her, too, although they have not declared their feelings to each other. Lucy Steele, a young woman of much lower social standing and education than Elinor, is visiting the Dashwoods. During a lighthearted conversation, another visitor makes it known that Elinor secretly has affection for Edward. Lucy reacts in a way that causes Elinor to think she knows Edward well. Elinor is quite surprised and wonders what their connection is. The real surprise, however—both for Elinor and the reader—is yet to come. One afternoon, Lucy seeks out Elinor to take a walk with her so they can talk.

"You will think my question an odd one, I dare say," said Lucy, "but pray, are you personally acquainted with your sister-in-law's mother, Mrs. Ferrars?"

Elinor did think the question a very odd one, and her countenance expressed it, as she answered that she had never seen Mrs. Ferrars.

"Indeed!" replied Lucy; "I wonder at that, for I thought you must have seen her at Norland sometimes. Then perhaps you cannot tell me what sort of a woman she is?"

"No," returned Elinor, cautious of giving her real opinion of Edward's mother, and not very desirous of satisfying what seemed impertinent curiosity. "I know nothing of her."

"I am sure you think me very strange, for inquiring about her in such a way," said Lucy, eyeing Elinor attentively as she spoke; "but perhaps there may be reasons—I wish I might venture; but however I hope you will do me the justice of believing that I do not mean to be impertinent."

Elinor made her a civil reply, and they walked on a few minutes in silence. It was broken by Lucy, who renewed the subject again by saying with some hesitation:

"I cannot bear to have you think me impertinently curious; I am sure I would rather do anything in the world than be thought so by a person whose good opinion is so well worth having as yours. And I am sure I should not have the smallest fear of trusting you; indeed I should be very glad of your advice how to manage in such an uncomfortable situation as I am; but however there is no occasion to trouble you. I am sorry you do not happen to know Mrs. Ferrars."

"I am sorry I do not," said Elinor in great astonishment, "if it could be of any use to you to know my opinion of her. But really, I never understood that you were at all connected with that family, and therefore I am a little surprised, I confess, at so serious an inquiry into her character."

"I dare say you are, and I am sure I do not at all wonder at it. But if I dared tell you all, you would not be so much surprised. Mrs. Ferrars is certainly nothing to me at present—but the time may come—how soon it will come must depend upon herself—when we may be very intimately connected."

She looked down as she said this, amiably bashful, with only one side-glance at her companion to observe its effect on her. "Good heavens!" cried Elinor, "what do you mean? Are you acquainted with Mr. Robert Ferrars? Can you be?" And she did not feel much delighted with the idea of such a sister-in-law.

"No," replied Lucy, "not with Mr. Robert Ferrars—I never saw him in my life; but," fixing her eyes upon Elinor, "with his elder brother."

What felt Elinor at that moment? Astonishment, that would have been as painful as it was strong had not an immediate disbelief of the assertion attended it. She turned towards Lucy in silent amazement, unable to divine the reason or object of such a declaration; and though her complexion varied, she stood firm in incredulity, and felt in no danger of an hysterical fit or a swoon.

"You may well be surprised," continued Lucy; "for, to be sure, you could have had no idea of it before; for I dare say he never dropped the smallest hint of it to you or any of your family; because it was always meant to be a great secret, and I am sure has been faithfully kept so by me to this hour. Not a soul of all my relations know of it but Anne, and I never should have mentioned it to you, if I had not felt the greatest dependence in the world upon your secrecy; and I really thought my behaviour in asking so many questions about Mrs. Ferrars must seem so odd that it ought to be explained. And I do not think Mr. Ferrars can be displeased when he knows I have trusted you, because I know he has the highest opinion in the world of all your family, and looks upon yourself and the other Miss Dashwoods quite as his own sisters." She paused.

Elinor for a few moments remained silent. Her astonishment at what she heard was at first too great for words; but at length forcing herself to speak, and to speak cautiously, she said with a calmness of manner which tolerably well concealed her surprise and solicitude—"May I ask if your engagement is of long standing?"

"We have been engaged these four years."

"Four years?"

"Yes."

Elinor, though greatly shocked, still felt unable to believe it.

"I did not know," said she, "that you were even acquainted till the other day."

"Our acquaintance, however, is of many years' date.

He was under my uncle's care, you know, a considerable while."

"Your uncle!"

"Yes; Mr. Pratt. Did you never hear him talk of Mr. Pratt?"

"I think I have," replied Elinor, with an exertion of spirits which increased with her increase of emotion.

"He was four years with my uncle, who lives at Longstaple, near Plymouth. It was there our acquaintance begun, for my sister and me was often staying with my uncle, and it was there our engagement was formed though not till a year after he had quitted as a pupil; but he was almost always with us afterwards. I was very unwilling to enter into it, as you may imagine, without the knowledge and approbation of his mother; but I was too young and loved him too well to be so prudent as I ought to have been. Though you do not know him as well as me, Miss Dashwood, you must have seen enough of him to be sensible he is very capable of making a woman sincerely attached to him."

"Certainly," answered Elinor, without knowing what she said; but after a moment's reflection, she added with revived security of Edward's honour and love, and her companion's falsehood—"Engaged to Mr. Edward Ferrars! I confess myself so totally surprised at what you tell me, that really—I beg your pardon; but surely there must be some mistake of person or name. We cannot mean the same Mr. Ferrars."

"We can mean no other," cried Lucy, smiling. "Mr. Edward Ferrars, the eldest son of Mrs. Ferrars of Park Street, and brother of your sister-in-law, Mrs. John Dashwood, is the person I mean; you must allow that I am not likely to be deceived as to the name of the man on whom all my happiness depends."

"It is strange," replied Elinor, in a most painful perplexity, "that I should never have heard him even mention your name."

"No; considering our situation, it was not strange. Our

first care has been to keep the matter secret. You knew nothing of me or my family, and therefore there could be no occasion for ever mentioning my name to you; and as he was always particularly afraid of his sister's suspecting anything, that was reason enough for his not mentioning it."

She was silent. Elinor's security sunk; but her self-command did not sink with it.

"Four years you have been engaged," said she with a firm voice.

"Yes; and heaven knows how much longer we may have to wait. Poor Edward! It puts him quite out of heart." Then taking a small miniature from her pocket she added, "To prevent the possibility of mistake, be so good as to look at this face. It does not do him justice, to be sure, but yet I think you cannot be deceived as to the person it was drew for. I have had it above these three years."

She put it into her hands as she spoke, and when Elinor saw the painting whatever other doubts her fear of a too hasty decision or her wish of detecting falsehood might suffer to linger in her mind, she could have none of its being Edward's face. She returned it almost instantly, acknowledging the likeness.

Exploration Points

1. What is the subtext of the conversation between these two women? How does the subtexted meaning fit with their action objectives?

   Lucy's initial action objective for the scene: to convince Elinor to stay away from Edward. Elinor's initial objective: to discover how Lucy is acquainted with Edward.

   Lucy first speaks of Mrs. Ferrars in order to bring up the topic of Edward. When Elinor says she knows nothing of Mrs. Ferrars, which could close the subject, Lucy's action objective becomes: to keep this conversation about Mrs. Ferrars going. She asks Elinor not to think her impertinent for inquiring about Mrs. Ferrars, then hints at reasons for her inquiry. Her subtext: *You don't want to end this conversation just yet, Elinor. I have things to tell you.* Unfortunately for Lucy, Elinor still doesn't take the bait. So Lucy must try again, once more bringing up the subject of Mrs. Ferrars. This time she does more than hint, telling Elinor she and Mrs. Ferrars may become intimately connected. When Elinor still fails to understand, Lucy alleges that she's engaged to Edward, not his brother, Robert.

Elinor's action objective immediately becomes: to convince herself of Edward's steadfastness. She first stares in silent amazement, then questions Lucy about the engagement at length. Subtext: *I don't believe you; you're lying.* Lucy's new action objective is: to prove she is in fact engaged to Edward. She mentions how she and Edward met through her uncle. Her subtext: *You'd better believe me.* Elinor, unable to refute these arguments, suggests that perhaps they are not talking about the same man. Subtext: *I know Edward loves me. He cannot possibly be the man of whom you speak.* Lucy responds with proof that they are, indeed, discussing the same man. Her subtext: *It's time to stop your denial.* Elinor, still unable to believe it, says she can't understand why Edward has never mentioned Lucy. Subtext: *I still do not believe you.* Lucy replies that Edward wanted to keep the engagement secret. Subtext: *You're running out of arguments, Elinor. Face the facts.*

Elinor still sounds unconvinced. Lucy pulls out the picture of Edward to "prevent the possibility of mistake" and places it in Elinor's hands. Subtext: *Look upon the face of the man who's mine, not yours.* Elinor is faced with the painful truth. Her new action objective: to hide her grief. She apparently keeps a calm voice as she admits it is Edward, but by returning the picture "almost instantly," she betrays her subtext: *I cannot bear to look at it.*

2. Delineate the description of Thought, Inflection, Movement, and Expression that convey the underlying communication of both women. Which is used most often? Which is used least?

Jane Austen uses mostly Thought to explain Elinor's reactions. Since the scene is told from Elinor's point of view, we are privy to her thoughts only.

Inflection is used numerous times. First Elinor is said to make a "civil reply" to Lucy. A short time later Elinor says something in "great astonishment" and later cries "Good heavens!" In a cautious and calm voice that hides her surprise she asks Lucy how long she's been engaged to Edward. Finally, she firmly states "Four years you have been engaged," her inflection implying more of a probing question since she still does not believe it.

Movement and Expression are less often used to convey Elinor's subtext. When Lucy first refers to Edward, Elinor turns to her "in silent amazement"—a mixture of both Movement and Expression. In the same sentence we're told "her complexion varied," another use of Expression. And later, Elinor is said to show "painful perplexity" as she makes a reply. The perplexity could show through both Inflection and Expression. Elinor's final movement, her instant return of the picture, packs the most emotion because it so clearly betrays her subtext.

Since Austen remains in Elinor's point of view, she cannot use Thought to convey Lucy's meaning. Instead, she uses Expression almost exclusively. Lucy's eyes tell us much. In fact, it is through a mere glance that Lucy first reveals she has ulterior motives for the conversation. When she first mentions her engagement to Edward, she looks down shyly, but glances sideways at Elinor to gauge the reaction. At other times, again when making statements about Edward, Lucy looks keenly at Elinor to observe her response. Lucy's one Movement provides the climax of this interchange. She puts the picture of Edward in Elinor's hands, forcing Elinor to accept the fact that they are talking about the same man.

FROM
Slow Waltz in Cedar Bend
by Robert James Waller

Setting: Iowa, present day. Middle-aged college professor Michael Tillman has met another professor's wife, Jellie Braden, and is immediately attracted to her, as she is to him. On the surface, they become friends, Jellie dropping by Michael's office to chat on a regular basis. But, in fact, they both want a much different relationship. Then Jellie's husband tells Michael that he and Jellie will be living in London while he teaches the next semester there. Michael can't bear to think of not seeing Jellie for that length of time. An hour after he hears the news, Jellie stops by his office to visit.

"Hi, motorcycle man. How's the war?"

"The war is being won, Jellie. I'm whipping the students up the hills of December, and victory is mine, or will be in less than two weeks." She stood in the doorway instead of coming in and flopping down on a chair the way she usually did.

"Sorry I haven't been by to say hello. I've been getting ready for my final exams, and Jim said he told you about the London trip. What a mess, finding a house sitter on short notice, getting bills paid and things set up at the bank. I've been running for days with no letup. What are you going to do over the holidays? Any big plans?"

"No, not much at all. It's too cold to crank up the bike and ride it someplace. I'll probably try to finish the paper I'm doing on comparing complex structures so I can present it at the fall meetings. Get my trimonthly haircut, spend a few days with my mother out in Custer over Christmas. Other than that, watch the snow fall, I guess, and listen to the Miles Davis tapes I ordered while I spruce up my lectures for the class I'll be covering for Jim. My notes in that area are a little yellowed. It'll go by pretty fast, it always does." He wanted to say he'd be thinking about her every other minute, but he didn't.

"Sounds pretty low key. No special Christmas wishes?"

He looked at the ceiling for a moment, struggling, trying to pull himself up and out of a self-indulgent funk. Michael had wishes all right, but nothing he could talk about. He recovered and leaned back in his chair, fingers locked behind his head, forcing a little grin. "Well, sometime I'd like a leather belt with Orville tooled on the back. Used to be a guy in Custer had one, and I thought it was pretty neat when I was a kid."

Jellie grinned back. "Only you, Michael, of all the people I know, would say something like that. It's almost surreal."

"Well, life is surreal, Jellie. Except for Orville. He didn't dwell on those things, just drove his grain truck and whistled a lot."

"I think Orville had it all worked out. I'd like to hear more about him, but I've got to run. I'll try to stop in before we leave. Take care, Michael, and say hello to Orville if you see him. Ask if he'll write a self-help book for the rest of the world."

Exploration Points

1. What is the subtext of this conversation? How does the subtext fit with the characters' initial action objectives for the scene?

   Jellie approaches this scene with the initial action objective: to see how Michael is handling the news that she's leaving. Michael's action objective is: to hide his dismay at the news.

   Of course, Jellie cannot ask him directly. So she opens with the question, "How's the war?" Subtext: *How's the war inside you? How are you going to be without me here?*

   Michael responds with answers about his work, saying the war is being won. Subtext: *I'm managing.*

   Jellie apologizes that she hasn't been by because of all her preparations for the trip, weaving in the fact that her husband told her he'd informed Michael about it. Subtext: *I'm aware that you know I'm leaving*. Then she inquires what he'll do over the holidays. Subtext: *I'm afraid you'll be so lonely. What will you do with yourself?*

Michael responds that he won't be doing much. Subtext: *I'm going to be miserable and bored*.

Here, Jellie can't help but bait him a little. She asks if he has any "special Christmas wishes." Subtext: *I know you'll miss me. I just wish you could admit it*. Her question invokes the intended emotion within Michael. He responds with a silly answer about a leather belt. Subtext: *I can't begin to talk about what I really want, so I'm going to get you on another subject*. The subtext of Jellie's response: *You're so funny and entertaining, Michael. It's part of why I'm attracted to you*.

Michael picks up on a word Jellie used, replying that life is surreal, except for Orville. Subtext: *This game we're playing is unbelievable, isn't it? Sometimes I wish I could be as simple-minded as a guy like Orville. This would never happen to him*. Jellie understands Michael completely. "Orville had it all worked out," she says. "Ask if he'll write a self-help book." Subtext: *How are we ever going to continue this way?*

2. Review a scene you've written in which subtexting could be better used to increase dramatic tension. Rewrite where necessary.

Moving On

All the samples above depict how subtexting enriches dialogue and deepens characterization. We've seen how subtexted conversation, while calm on the surface, can be roiling with underlying emotion. Now we turn our focus to these emotions themselves. How do we portray them to their utmost? How do we infuse in our characters three-dimensional qualities while remaining true to their basic personality traits? How do we create characters who will tug at readers' hearts?

Let's look now at Secret #4, Coloring Passions.

Coloring Passions

ACTOR'S TECHNIQUE:

To portray human passions to their fullest, an actor must focus not on the overall passion itself but on all the individual *colors* that make up its palette. For example, love under varied circumstances can encompass such feelings as embarrassment, shame, jealousy, anger, fear. The more sweeping the passion, the more varied and even contradictory these feelings will be.

NOVELIST'S ADAPTATION:

Just as in acting, three-dimensional characters in novels require three-dimensional emotions, for in real life no person is entirely one thing. When you focus not on the general passion of your character, but on its component parts, its opposite, and its growth, your character will deepen in richness and represent human nature to its fullest.

The Challenge of Coloring Passions

In this chapter we face the daunting challenge of how to portray our characters' passions with all the vivid hues they would boast in real life.

This challenge applies to all writers, regardless of fiction genre. No matter what kind of story you write, your readers will crave characters that reflect human passions in all their shades of color. Whether they realize it or not, when readers approach a book they are looking for that "slice of life" that represents the human condition and all the wonderful and terrible passions it comprises. They want to be transported and entertained, and at the same time perhaps gain some new insights about life. If we're going to meet all these expectations, no "in general" passions for our characters will suffice. One-dimensional characters can't possibly entertain or shed new light on life's circumstances as well as characters who are bursting with passions that shimmer and sweep and curl around readers' shoulders like a familiar blanket. For it's with such passions that readers connect.

Stanislavsky's teaching on portraying passions to their fullest is one of his most eye-opening in terms of creating three-dimensional characters. In his book *Creating a Role,* he is scathing in describing actors who portray passions "in general." As an example, he mentions the operatic tenor whose specialty is to play "love." (Stanislavsky was known to be hard on opera stars, as their acting was often wooden and pretentious.) This particular tenor's idea of love comprised such gestures as pressing a hand to his heart, striking thoughtful poses, kissing his leading lady, proclaiming his desire for her, dreamily staring into the distance, sighing with melancholy, and so on. How naively one-sided and simple, Stanislavsky said disdainfully, to portray love as merely love. Or to portray hatred as merely hatred, jealousy as merely jealousy.

We can picture Stanislavsky's description of this "prettified" tenor with his "hair curled to look like an angel" and laugh as we imagine his old-fashioned antics. Trouble is, sometimes our own characters aren't as far removed from this vision as we'd like to think.

As we look at the technique of coloring passions, keep in mind that "passions" will refer to two different things: (1) traits, and (2) emotions.

In Secret #1, Personalizing, we saw that traits spring directly from your character's inner values. For example, because of upbringing and experiences, your character may have an inner value of avoiding controversy and seeking quiet. From this inner value could spring the trait of gentleness. Or perhaps your character has an inner value of trusting in God to take care of things. From this could spring the trait of stability in the face of trouble. These traits have just as much tendency as emotions—if not more—to force characters into a one-dimensional level. What's to keep a gentle character from being nothing but gentle? What's to keep a character who trusts in God from being always trusting, always stable? Or for that matter, what's to keep a mean, harsh, or selfish character from always being so?

In order to get the most out of this chapter, you should already know some of your character's traits. These traits should have risen to the surface during the personalizing process. If you are unclear about these traits, I urge you to re-visit the personalizing process in Secret #1.

As for emotions, their origins also lie in part within your character's inner values. Blend these inner values with your character's Desire, then add opposition to that Desire (conflict). Result: instant emotions. Depending upon the circumstances, they may be minor or all-encompassing, but they will certainly be present.

> (Inner Values + Desire) + Conflict = Emotion

We can learn to color the passions—both the traits and emotions—of our characters with their full range of hues by taking a fascinating three-part journey through a passion itself.

Part I: Find the Passion's Components

Stanislavsky likens a human passion to a necklace of beads. Standing back from the necklace, you might think it appears to have a yellow cast or a green or red one. But come closer, and you can see all the tiny beads that create that overall appearance. If the necklace appears yellow, many beads will be yellow, but in various shades. And a few may be green or blue or even black. In the same way, human passions are made up of many smaller and varied feelings—sometimes even contradictory feelings—that together form the "cast" or color of a certain passion. So, if you want to portray a passion to its utmost, you must focus not on the passion itself, but on its varied components.

For example, in my novel *Cast a Road Before Me*, twenty-four-year-old Jessie falls in love with Lee, a man a few years her senior. As the story unfolds, there is no doubt that this love is growing. But how does Jessie portray the passion of love? She first meets Lee with trepidation, then keeps a cynical eye on him to ensure he adheres to a certain promise. She argues with him, ignores him, refuses to call him back, goes on a date with him, and kisses him. She also judges his actions, thinks ill of him, tells him he's wonderful, embraces his family, sticks by him in tragedy, plans to leave him, judges him some more, says she loves him, fights with him, pledges never to forgive him, opposes him in further tragedy, ultimately forgives him. All of these occurrences are but a few of the varied "beads" that, when strung together, create the "necklace" of Jessie's love for Lee.

Outside of the context of the story, you may think these beads are so varied because Jessie is a volatile young woman whose emotions run the gamut of height and depth in a single day. Not so; she's really quite level-headed. Actually, Lee is the volatile one. These beads are varied not because of Jessie's capriciousness, but because the conflicts that arise in opposition to her Desire and inner values naturally lead her to such reactions. My goal was to build a character who appears believable and empathetic—and also very much in love—even as she treats Lee in such varied ways.

How do we discover these kinds of varied colors or "beads" that comprise a character's passion? Here is the key:

> Create scenes of conflict that will allow the different colors of a passion to appear.

When you are seeking the various colors of a character's trait or emotion, look to these pieces of information about your character and story for ideas to create conflict:

- inner values
- Desire
- the progression from Distancing to Denial to Devastation
- inner values and Desires of other characters
- your story's answering end

Since conflict is the dynamic that keeps a story moving, view these pieces of information in light of their potential opposition to one another. Under what circumstances could a character's inner values conflict with her Desire? In pursuing their own Desires, what actions could other characters take that oppose her? Where in the progression of the Four Ds could beads of the most difference in color be placed? Answers to these kinds of questions will help you create conflict that will prompt your character to show the various components of an emotion or trait.

But in some novels, portraying the components of a character's passion isn't enough. As Stanislavsky notes, the greater the passion, the greater all the colors that compose it. To build characters with the most sweeping of passions, look to Part II.

Part II: Find the Passion's Opposite

Colors are best displayed against an opposing background. Place a pearl necklace against a white dress and the colors will blend together. Rather than enhancing the effect of the necklace through its similar color, the dress actually deadens it. Place that same necklace against a black dress and two results occur. First, the pearls stand out in a dynamic way. Second, they appear whiter.

So it is with human passions. When a novel requires that you portray your character's emotion or trait to its fullest, that you show its overall color at its most brilliant, you'll need to include its opposite as well as its components. If your character is harsh, find what is gentle in him. If she's selfish, find her generous side. If she's self-confident, find her point of self-doubt. If he's emotionally strong, find his weakness.

Picture the evil character of an abusive single mother. She kicks her daughter and beats her son with a belt. She screams and taunts and belittles them both. Later we see her cuddle a sick kitten. This tender care of an animal in no way diminishes our sense of her brutality toward her own children. Quite the reverse; her brutality is heightened by sheer comparison.

The opposite of a passion is easy enough to identify, but finding a way to portray it with believability is something else again. After all, we want a character with colored passions, not a wishy-washy one. We need to carefully seek the right opportunity, the right scene that will allow this opposite to naturally show itself. Here we need to treat a character's traits and emotions a little differently.

> To find the most opportunities for portraying the opposite of a *trait*, look *within the character*.

These three steps will help you create the kind of vivid scene you're looking for:

1. Trace the trait back to the inner value of your character that gave rise to it.
2. Find a second inner value of your character.
3. Ask yourself in what situation you could place your character so that the second inner value conflicts with the first, thereby producing the trait's opposite.

For example, let's say your character has an inner value of empathy toward people. This gives rise to the trait of always allowing others the benefit of the doubt. She's slow to "get her back up," so to speak. If someone slights her, she shrugs it off, thinking the person is just having a bad day. A second inner value of hers involves the good treatment of customers as a smart way to do business. This value was instilled in her by her mother, who owns a successful bookstore. The character has often helped out behind the counter and has seen first-hand the positive financial results of meeting a customer's needs with efficiency and cheer. To her way of thinking, the customer is absolutely king.

Now, how to pit these two inner values, which normally fit hand in glove, against each other? One answer: make your character the customer in a poorly managed store. Up the ante a bit and place her in a real hurry. She hastens to the counter of this store with an item to purchase. The young boy behind the counter is lax, doesn't make eye contact, and continues chatting blithely with his coworker. Your character waits, then clears her throat to no avail. Judgment—not empathy—rises within her. As far as she is concerned, this boy deserves to be fired on the spot. If he were in her mother's store, she fumes to herself, he *would* be fired. He's not just having a bad day; he's making *her* day bad. *Nothing* could excuse such behavior. By the time your character finally is helped, she's become terse, tight-lipped, and unfriendly. When she flounces out of the store, the boy behind the counter may well turn to his coworker and mutter, "Don't you just hate people like that?!"

We can look to the character of Finny in John Knowles's classic novel *A Separate Peace* as another example of trait opposites. Finny is described as a charming sixteen-year-old at the Devon School who seems to get away with anything, a "student who combined a calm ignorance of the rules with a winning urge to be good, who seemed to love the school truly and deeply, and never more than when he was breaking the regulations, a model boy who was most comfortable in the truant's corner." In other words, Finny possessed the trait of making up his own rules. Finny was also honest. "Everything he said was true and sincere; Finny always said what he happened to be thinking, and if this stunned people then he was surprised."

In making up his own rules, Finny often shows himself to be a great and fearless athlete. In the opening of the book, Finny decides that he and his friends should climb a huge tree by the river, then jump from its branches into the water—a feat that was considered crazy by his school chums and was absolutely against school rules. Of course Finny jumps first, urging his friends to follow. Gene, the novel's narrator, reluctantly jumps next. Elwin declares Gene's jump better than Finny's. Finny cordially replies, "Don't start awarding prizes until you've passed the course. The tree is waiting." Elwin refuses to jump, as do the other students. Finny declares to Gene, "It's you, pal. Just you and me."

In another scene, Finny breaks the school record for 100-yard freestyle swimming, with Gene, holding the stopwatch, as his only witness. Finny is not a practiced swimmer, which makes his feat all the more sensational. But Finny stuns Gene by declaring that his record-breaking swim will remain a secret. What's more, Finny refuses to swim the event again publicly so that he can officially break the record. Gene can hardly believe it. The bronze plaque bearing the name of A. Hopkins Parker as record-holder for this swim will remain hanging in the school halls—a lie after Finny's achievement. Yet honest Finny chooses to let the lie stand.

What has happened? Finny's trait of making up his own rules has come into direct opposition with his trait of honesty, and the first trait wins. "Swimming is screwy anyway," he tells Gene. "The only real swimming is in the ocean." Apparently, to Finny's unique thought processes, proving his swimming prowess by conforming to a standard set of rules and regulations for breaking a record is something he just can't do. Remember, he plays outside the rules. Usually, this behavior displays his athletic abilities. But even when it does not, he still chooses to live by his own rules. And he chooses to live this way even if it requires that he is less than completely honest about his achievement.

By placing Finny in this situation and forcing two of his major traits to come head-to-head, John Knowles succeeds in showing us a new depth to Finny's character.

> To find the most opportunities for portraying the opposite of an *emotion*, look to *other characters*.

What actions might other characters in your novel take that would oppose the first character so strongly that she would be pushed to the opposite emotion?

For example, let's say your character, a middle-aged woman, is deeply in love with her husband. In the last few months, however, he's begun to treat her badly, staying out late at night with no explanation, ignoring her needs. She's afraid he's having an affair. Still, she's been patient, often saying how much she loves him and trying her best to meet all his needs. Finally she decides this has continued long enough. She must woo her husband back. One night she makes a special dinner for him and squeezes herself into a sexy dress. She has extracted from him the absolute promise that he'll come home immediately from work. But he fails to arrive on time. She waits. The dinner grows cold. She grows cold in her skimpy dress and adds a sweater. Takes off her high heels. An hour passes. She paces and paces, looking out the window, worrying, wondering. Still he doesn't show. In time she cries, then cries some more. After a while the tears dry up, and then she grows angry. She vows she won't love him anymore. He doesn't deserve her! She stomps around the room, throwing at his imagined form all the awful accusations she's held back over the past few months. Finally she sinks into the couch, spent. Only then does she hear his car in the driveway. Her anger rises again. She faces the front door, waiting, standing stiffly, her breath ragged and her makeup smeared. He eases into the room carrying a dozen red roses. Seeing her expression, he stops in his tracks. Meekly, he holds the roses out to her, saying, "I love you." Two hours ago she would have accepted them with tears in her eyes. Now she glares at him with pure, unadulterated hatred. With one sweep of her arm, she knocks the roses out of his hands and onto the floor.

Any doubts this woman loves her husband?

Just as love can reveal itself through hate, given the right circumstances, so joy can reveal itself through sorrow, courage through fear, trust through doubt. The trick is to create the scene, or a series of scenes, that allows your character this opposite's natural unfolding. Like the pearl necklace against a black dress, your character's emotion will be deepened and enhanced by the very presence of its opposite.

To sum up, in coloring passions we must present components and perhaps even an opposite of the trait or emotion. But how do we introduce these varied colors in a logical and coherent manner?

Part III: Find the Passion's Growth

A passion's growth can apply to both individual scenes and your novel as a whole. If you were to write the scene of the unhappy wife and her tardy husband, her transition from love to a moment of hate would need to be portrayed in its natural progression. The reader would need to see in full all the colors implied in the description above. Your character would first feel anticipation, maybe even excitement. When her husband doesn't arrive on time, she would experience disappointment, then anxiety, questioning, and fear. Then anger at her husband, followed by anger at herself for loving him. Then defeat, and finally fury as she realizes that he expects a lousy bunch of flowers to make up for all his unforgivable actions. At this point she can momentarily hate him. But only because she's gone through all the colors, or emotions, between love and hate. Readers will not only believe this natural progression, they'll empathize with it, for likely they too have experienced the colored passions of opposites.

The principle of growth for a scene holds true for the novel as a whole. If your character is fearful at the beginning of your story, and by the end has found courage, we need to see this process and all its varied colors in a natural order that accurately represents life. Too often authors—particularly first-time authors—make their characters turn suddenly, one event moving them from darkness to light, or light to darkness. This is simply not the nature of human passions. To believe a change from fear to courage, a reader must perceive from the outset a tiny bead here and there of potential bravery. These may be almost imperceptible, but they will be present. Then, slowly, more "bravery" beads are added as the "fearful" beads decrease in number.

A little more, and a little more, until the shade of the entire neck-lace begins to change. What's more, somewhere along the way the color of each individual "courage" bead intensifies. Then perhaps a few "fearful" beads are added back in, and the shade becomes difficult to determine. Then more "courage" beads are returned, and still more and more added until finally the change is complete.

These changes won't occur at an even pace throughout your book. Certain key events will prompt the addition of numerous beads at once, whether the positive ones of courage or the setbacks of returning fear. The crisis and climax of your story may involve a relatively major change for your character. Readers expect that. But they will only believe such change when they've seen the natural progression of colors that must precede it. Being human themselves and having experienced their own passions, they will inherently know if your story is true to human nature or if it's not.

And what is fiction about if not the true portrayal of human emotions? That is the goal authors should strive for most. Sadly, it's the goal many of us fail to attain.

Authors spend a lifetime learning how to master the portrayal of passions. In our quest we must come to know the passions intimately. We need to learn all the varied colors of passions' components and opposites, and to understand their natural growth and change. To gain such knowledge we turn to people around us and to ourselves. (In the final secret, Emotion Memory, we'll discover ways to build upon our personal knowledge of passions.) As an author, you should constantly study human nature—observing, noting, filing away impressions. Then, armed with all the knowledge you have gathered, you will be able to color the passions of your characters in a believ-able and emotionally realistic way.

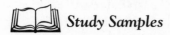 *Study Samples*

Rather than using individual scenes, each sample includes excerpts from various scenes of a novel that together show the components of passions and their natural progression. In the first sample a man's life-passion is completely and irrevocably lost to him. In the second we see the widely ranging colors of love.

FROM
Les Miserables
by Victor Hugo

Setting: France, early 1800s. The formidable and implacable Javert, a policeman, follows only one path in life—that of the law. Nothing else matters, not compassion, never mercy. The law is the law, and it demands judgment and retribution. This inner value colors everything he does and, in fact, becomes his very definition.

Javert thinks he has committed an unpardonable offense in believing that the respected Mayor Monsieur Madeleine is Jean Valjean, the escaped convict whom he has sought for years to bring to justice. In Javert's mind, he himself must be punished. He visits Monsieur Madeleine and confesses his previous belief, declaring that he now knows he was wrong.

"Monsieur Mayor, there is one more thing to which I desire to call your attention."

"What is it?"

"It is that I ought to be dismissed."

Monsieur Madeleine arose. "Javert, you are a man of honour and I esteem you. You exaggerate your fault. I desire you to keep your place."

Javert looked at Monsieur Madeleine with his calm eyes, in whose depths it seemed that one beheld his conscience, unenlightened, but stern and pure, and said in a tranquil voice, "Monsieur Mayor, I cannot agree to that. As to exaggerating, I do not exaggerate. This is the way I reason. I have unjustly suspected you. That is nothing. It is our province to suspect, although it may be an abuse of our right to suspect our superiors. But without proofs and in a fit of anger, with revenge as my aim, I denounced you as a convict—you, a respectable man, a mayor and a magistrate. This is a serious matter, very serious. I have committed an offence against authority in your person, I who am the agent of authority. If one of my subordinates had done what I have, I would have pronounced him unworthy of the service, and sent him away."

All this was said in a tone of proud humility, a desperate and resolute tone, which gave an indescribably whimsical grandeur to this oddly honest man.

"We will see," said Monsieur Madeleine. And he held out his hand to him.

Javert started back and said fiercely, "Pardon, Monsieur Mayor, that should not be. A mayor does not give his hand to a spy." He added between his teeth, "Spy, yes; from the moment I abused the power of my position I have been nothing better than a spy!"

Then he bowed profoundly, and went towards the door.

Later in the book, Javert learns that Monsieur Madeleine is indeed Jean Valjean, and in the following scene Javert goes to arrest him. Valjean is in a hospital room, watching over Fantine, a sick young mother he's taken into his care.

One who did not know Javert could have divined nothing of what was going on, and would have thought his manner the most natural imaginable. He was cool, calm, grave; his grey hair lay perfectly smooth over his temples, and he ascended the stairway with his customary deliberation. But one who knew him thoroughly and examined him with attention would have shuddered. The buckle of his leather cravat, instead of being on the back of his neck, was under his left ear. This denoted an unheard-of agitation.

Javert was a complete character, without a wrinkle in his duty or his uniform, methodical with villains, riding with the buttons of his coat. For him to misplace the buckle of his cravat, he must have received one of those shocks which may well be the earthquakes of the soul. . . .

On reaching the room of Fantine, Javert turned the key, pushed open the door with the gentleness of a sick-nurse, or a police spy, and entered. . . . Fantine raised her eyes, saw him, and caused Monsieur Madeleine to turn around.

At the moment when the glance of Madeleine encountered that of Javert, Javert, without stirring, without moving, without approaching, became terrible. No human feeling can ever be so appalling as joy.

It was the face of a demon who had again found his victim.

Javert sends Jean Valjean to prison, but on a prisoner's ship, Valjean is thrown overboard and manages to escape. Years later Valjean becomes involved with a group of young revolutionaries because of the relationship between his adopted daughter, Cosette (the late Fantine's child), and Marius, one of the group's leaders. Javert, ever the policeman, is now in pursuit of these revolutionaries. Here, some of the radical young men catch him.

In a twinkling before Javert had had time to turn around, he was collared, thrown down, bound, searched. . . . The search finished, they raised Javert, tied his arms behind his back, and fastened him in the middle of the basement room. . . . Javert had not uttered a cry . . . he held up his head with the intrepid serenity of the man who has never lied.

Enjolras said, "You will be shot ten minutes before the barricade is taken."

Javert replied in the most imperious tone, "Why not immediately?"

"We are economising powder."

"Then do it with a knife."

The revolutionaries give Valjean the honor of shooting Javert, not knowing the history between these two men. Valjean drags the fettered Javert outside, where they are alone.

Jean Valjean put the pistol under his arm, and fixed upon Javert a look which had no need of words. "Javert, it is I."

Javert answered, "Take your revenge."

Jean Valjean took a knife out of his pocket, and opened it. . . . [He] cut the martingale which Javert had about his neck, then he cut the ropes which he had on his wrists, then, stooping down, he cut the cord which he had on his feet; and, rising, he said to him, "You are free."

Javert was not easily astonished. Still, complete master as he was of himself, he could not escape an emotion. He stood aghast and motionless.

Jean Valjean continued, "I don't expect to leave this place. Still, if by chance I should, I live, under the name of Fauchelevent, in the Rue de l'Homme Armé, Number Seven."

Javert repeated in an undertone, "Number seven." He buttoned his coat, restored the military stiffness between his shoulders, turned half around, folded his arms, supporting his chin with one hand, and walked off in the direction of the markets. Jean Valjean followed him with his eyes. After a few steps, Javert turned back, and cried to Jean Valjean, "You annoy me. Kill me rather."

Javert did not notice that his tone was more respectful toward Jean Valjean.

"Go away," said Jean Valjean.

Javert receded with slow steps.

Javert once more catches up with Valjean, this time as Valjean is trying to save the life of Marius, who is seriously wounded. Valjean asks Javert to allow him to take Marius home first before he is arrested. Javert relents, escorting Javert and the unconscious Marius to Javert's house. When the carriage driver complains of the blood left upon his seat, Javert pays for the damage. They reach Valjean's home.

"Very well," said Javert. "Go up," he added with a strange expression and as if he were making effort in speaking in such a way, "I will wait here for you."

Jean Valjean looked at Javert. This manner of proceeding was little in accordance with Javert's habits. . . .

On reaching the first story, he paused. . . . He leaned over the street. It is short, and the lamp lighted it from one end to the other. Jean Valjean was bewildered with amazement; there was nobody there.

Javert was gone.

Javert cannot understand—or accept—his own actions. He has let a prisoner, a violator of the law, go.

Javert made his way with slow steps from the Rue de l'Homme Armé. He walked with his head down, for the first time in his life, and, for the first time in his life as well, with his hands behind his back. . . . His whole person, slow and gloomy, bore the impress of anxiety. . . .

He took the shortest route towards the Seine, reached the Quai des Ormes, went along the quai. . . . This point of the Seine is dreaded by mariners. Nothing is more dangerous than this rapid. . . . Men who fall in there, one never sees again; the best swimmers are drowned.

Javert leaned both elbows on the parapé, with his chin in his hands, and while his fingers were clenched mechanically in the thickest of his whiskers, he reflected.

There had been a new thing, a revolution, a catastrophe in the depths of his being, and there was matter for self-examination.

Javert was suffering rightfully. . . . [He] felt that duty was growing weaker in his conscience, and he could not hide it from himself. . . . He saw before him two roads, both equally straight; but he saw two; and that terrified him—him, who had never in his life known but one straight line. And, bitter anguish, these two roads were contradictory. One of these two straight lines excluded the other. Which of the two was true?

His condition was inexpressible.

To owe life to a malefactor, to accept that debt and to pay it, to be, in spite of himself, on a level with a fugitive from justice, and to pay him for one service with another service; to allow him to say, "Go away," and to say to him in turn, "Be free"; to sacrifice duty, that general obligation, to personal motives, and to feel in these personal motives something general also, and perhaps superior; to betray society in order to be true to his own conscience; that all these absurdities should be realised and that they should be accumulated upon himself, this was by which he was prostrated. . . .

Where was he? He sought himself and found himself no longer.

Javert throws himself into the Seine and drowns.

Exploration Points

1. What are the different colors of Javert's passion for upholding the law?

   In the first scene the color is *self-deprecation*. Javert cannot forgive even himself when he feels he has done something unworthy of the law.

   In the second scene, Hugo shows us Javert's *amazement* at discovering that a man he'd esteemed could actually be a common criminal. In Javert's mind, a criminal will look and smell like a criminal. Hugo uses the misplaced buckle of Javert's cravat to show us his "unheard-of agitation." Then, the moment Javert lays eyes on Valjean, his amazement turns into cold, hard *vindication* as his expression shows "the face of a demon who had again found his victim."

When he is captured, Javert displays a *sadistic pride* as he urges the young men to kill him whatever way they can, thereby proving themselves to be the bloodthirsty criminals he perceives them to be.

The fourth scene is a turning point for Javert, for he is forced to look upon a "lawless" man as one who is upholding the law by allowing him to go free. Javert rapidly experiences one emotion after another. First he rests in his *stoicism* regarding his assumed fate in Valjean's hands: "Take your revenge." Then he shows severe shock at being set free. Recovering quickly, he repeats Valjean's address, displaying his *resolve* to uphold the law, regardless of what Valjean has done for him. Next he suffers *despondency* to the point where he prefers death to enduring the reality that his lifelong segregation of "good" and "bad" people has been so shaken.

When Javert lets Valjean go in the next scene, repaying the debt for his life, he shows *mercy* for the very first time. But then he is unable to live with the fact that he has been merciful to a criminal. He falls into utter *despair*, with suicide his only way out.

2. Can you find any inner value for Javert other than his value of law as ultimate authority? Do the components and opposite of his passion for the law keep him from being a one-dimensional character?

    Javert's inner value of the law as ultimate authority is his only value. As a result, he could have been a mere flat character. But he is too important to the story to be one-dimensional. Hugo manages a marvelous feat with this character through deftly employing his very single-mindedness. By coloring the passion of Javert as his inner value is slowly stripped away, Hugo presents him as a serious-minded character who experiences all the emotions that any human would feel, albeit centered around one lifelong pursuit. These emotions include even extreme happiness, frighteningly displayed in that masterful sentence: "No human feeling can ever be so appalling as joy." Yet when Javert's single inner value is completely, irrevocably gone, he is shown to be just what he is—a shallow and narrow-minded man who cannot see the truth that lies beyond his own twisted perception.

3. Is the progression of colors from components to opposite believable? Why or why not?

The progression is very believable. In fact, when Javert commits suicide, it seems his only option. Over and over again, even as he is displaying various colors of his passion, Javert proves his willingness to sacrifice himself for his belief. First we see this intent as he insists that Valjean, the supposed mayor, dismiss him from his position because he has "committed an offence against authority." Then twice we see him willing to die as martyr, at the hands of the revolutionaries and, later, Valjean. When Valjean lets him go, Javert still asks to die and finally leaves reluctantly. Even when he allows Valjean to escape in turn, Javert is obviously shaken that he would make such a choice: "'Go up,' he added with a strange expression and as if he were making effort in speaking in such a way." As Javert drags himself to the Seine we see all of the past colors of his one passion flowing together to create a dark and dismal picture. Javert has lost his one passion and therefore his reason to live. "He sought himself and found himself no longer."

FROM

Peachtree Road
by Anne Rivers Siddons

Setting: the wealthy Buckhead section of Atlanta, Georgia, beginning in the 1940s and ending in the 1980s. Sheppard Gibbs Bondurant III, known as Gibby or Shep, is torn between the love for his sweet friend since childhood, Sarah Cameron, and the heady, gut-wrenching, ever-beckoning love for his wild and "luminous" first cousin, Lucy Venable.

*In the first scene, Gibby and Lucy are twelve and ten, respec-
tively. Lucy and her mother have lived with Gibby's family for
two years, and the children are inseparable—until they fall into
trouble, and their parents impose a long separation on them.
Gibby is in his own room, hearing the screams of Lucy as she
wails, "I want Gibby! I want Gibby!" He wants to run to her but
knows he would only be dragged away.*

"Okay," I said under my breath, fiercely, and yet with a kind
of detached calmness. I was absolutely clear in my mind.
"Just all of you wait until I get big enough. None of you are
going to be able to stop me then. I'm going to take Lucy and
go far away from here, and you'll never see either one of us
anymore in the world. I don't care how long it takes, I'm
going to do it."

And I lay back on my rumpled little bed and folded my
arms under my head and began, in a kind of furious peace,
that long wait.

*Gibby and Lucy are now teenagers, still living in the same house.
At dinner, Gibby has just announced his decision to leave Atlanta
to attend Princeton University. Lucy yells at him that he can't do
that, then runs from the room, crying.*

Lucy was still crying hard when I went up to her room at
ten that night, and she would not let me come in.

"Go away," she sobbed. "I don't want to see your face. I
hate you! You promised, and you broke your promise!"

"Come on, Lucy, let me in," I called softly, rapping on
the door. "What did I promise? Not to stay here and go to
school, I didn't. You knew about Princeton; I told you a long
time ago. You saw the letter last year. . . ."

"I didn't think you'd really do it," she said, in a voice
thick and hopeless with abandonment. "I thought you were
just fooling around about it. I never thought you really
meant to leave."

"But you said—"

"I DON'T CARE WHAT I SAID! YOU PROMISED ME YOU WOULD TAKE CARE OF ME FOREVER AND YOU'RE BREAKING YOUR PROMISE!" she shrieked, and there followed a loud thud, where she had thrown something heavy against the door. I was suddenly infinitely weary and sad, and I simply did not think I could cope with Lucy any longer on this night.

At a high school dance, Lucy shows up drunk and disheveled, demanding the last dance with Gibby, even though social etiquette calls for him to dance with the girl he brought—his sweetheart, Sarah.

"Sarah won't mind, Gibby," she said, and this time she did slur just a little, and rocked on her high heels so that she had to put out one hand to steady herself against my arm. "Sarah'll wait for us to finish. Good old Sarah. Sarah'll just sit all quiet like a little old puppy dog and wait for us. . . ."

She locked her arms around my neck and sagged against me, so that I was forced to hold her to prevent her from slipping to the floor. I looked at Sarah desperately over Lucy's head; her face was scarlet, but it was still and composed. . . .

"That's right," Lucy said in a singsong voice, her eyes closed, smiling, swaying. "You're a nice girl, Sarah; go on home with your big brother and let me dance with Shep—"

Rage flooded me coldly and fully then. I took Lucy by her upper arms and thrust her away from me so suddenly and sharply that her head bounced on her neck, and she opened her eyes and looked at me in the old simple, lost, Lucy bewilderment. I felt the traitorous twist begin in my heart, but the rage was stronger.

"Stand up, Lucy," I said. "I have this dance with Sarah, and I'm going to dance with her, and then I'm going to take her home."

Gibby and Sarah plan to marry. But Lucy stands always in their way, demanding Gibby's attention. After leaving Sarah suddenly to fly across country and extract Lucy from another mess, Gibby returns a week later to hear that Sarah has announced her engagement to one of his oldest friends, Charlie Gentry. After some days pass, he confronts Sarah and Charlie.

The bedroom door opened and Sarah came out and stood in front of me and looked so searchingly into my face that I thought I would drown under the endless amber look, or faint from it. . . . She leaned a little toward me, but she did not touch me. I didn't think I could have borne that.

"I have to matter to somebody as much as he does to me, Shep, or I'm totally devalued," she said. . . . "I saw when you went out there to get Lucy that I didn't to you, and I never would. It would mean everything to me if you could understand how I feel."

I abandoned myself to the rage. It was a feeling, almost, of luxury, of satiation; orgasmic. I had never felt it before, not with my mother or father, not even with Lucy. There was in it, under the sure and certain knowledge of unredeemable, irreparable damage, a kind of savage absolution. I laughed. It was an obscenity even in my own ears.

"You are wrong," I said to Sarah. "You are wrong about me, and you are wrong about that, and you are wrong about everything. You lied. It wasn't me you wanted. You wanted a pet dog, not a husband, and you got one. Enjoy it."

And I slammed out the door. . . .

In time Gibby forces himself to accept Sarah and Charlie's marriage, but his grief over Sarah still runs deep. One day Charlie visits him.

Charlie turned his face up to mine, and it was absolutely luminous. "I wanted you to know before anybody except Ben and Dorothy. It's really why I came by. Sarah wanted me to tell you. She's . . . we're going to have a baby. She's almost three months pregnant. It's due in June."

I felt stillness come down over me like a cast net. I

thought of Sarah's thinness, and the circles under her amber eyes, and of her words at the hospital: "I look like twelve miles of bad road. . . . But it's temporary."

"Congratulations, Papa," I said, and the tears that swam in my eyes, obscuring him for a moment, were for his joy as much as for the great, vast, windy emptiness that was the middle of me.

Gibby's mother is killed in a plane crash outside Paris along with many others from Buckhead. Gibby and Lucy go to Paris with others to claim the bodies. After a gruesome visit to five morgues, Gibby sits in his unlocked hotel room that night, Lucy in hers next door. Gibby is holding one of his mother's shoes recovered from the wreckage.

I turned off the light and sat holding my mother's shoe in my hand, and then, finally, in the heavy darkness, I wept, aloud and hard and painfully, like an utterly inconsolable child, not for what lay in the third morgue of Paris, but for what had laughed and danced in the beautiful, foolish shoe and for the hopeful best that would live on, now, in the name of Sarah's firstborn. I cried until I thought my chest would burst with the anguish; I could not stop; the tears poured and pounded on. I remember thinking, for the first time in my life, that it was possible to simply die of tears.

Sometime that night—I do not know when—Lucy came into the room and slipped into the bed with me. She was naked, and her body was long and light and silken and cool, and she pressed it around and against and under and over me, and her warm, sweet open mouth was against my face and hair and cheeks and eyelids and nose, and finally over my mouth, so that I sobbed directly into the breath of her, and then, simply and with a deep, deep flowering, she took me inside her, and rocked with me to a beat as old and deep and primal as the world, and was Lucy was Sarah was Lucy was Sarah, was Lucy was my mother was Sarah was Lucy, was the world, was the universe . . . and all that I had

not felt budded and bloomed and swelled and burst loose
and roared through me and she took it into herself, and I was
freed.

Exploration Points

1. Review each scene. What colors of Gibby's passion of love for
    Lucy does each portray? How does his love change from the first
    scene to the last?

    When he is twelve, Gibby shows *fierce determination* to be with
    Lucy when he is grown, telling himself that no one will stand in
    his way. As he tries to talk to Lucy about his leaving for college,
    Gibby experiences a *sad weariness* due to the demands that she's
    already placing upon him. Then at the dance, Gibby feels *shame*
    that leads to *rage,* and the rage outweighs his sense of being
    traitorous to Lucy. She is not only shaming him, she is shaming
    Sarah, and that he cannot allow.

    Although Lucy is not present when Gibby confronts Sarah
    and Charlie, and again when Charlie relays the news of Sarah's
    pregnancy, Gibby's love for Lucy still drives the scenes. In both
    of these scenes he faces the *devastation* of realizing that his
    fascination for the volatile Lucy has cost him a life with the
    woman who has been loyal to him and could have brought him
    so much joy.

    In the last scene of our example, Gibby first faces *desolation*
    at his abandonment and loneliness. He has lost Lucy, Sarah, and
    his mother. When Lucy finally meets him in the moment of his
    need, he experiences emotional *release* and then freedom.

2. Take a closer look at one of your own characters. How can you
    use the secret of coloring passions to deepen his or her charac-
    terization?

Moving On

From the wide expanse of coloring passions, we turn now to the actor's secret that will help you breathe life and believability into individual scenes. We'll learn how the various unique dynamics of your character—Desire, inner values, mannerisms, and passions— flow together to create the character's actions in times of conflict. Once again, to discover outer action, we look inside—to Secret #5, Inner Rhythm.

Inner Rhythm

ACTOR'S TECHNIQUE

Beneath an actor's external movements lies the internal "movement" of emotion. This *inner rhythm*, when used correctly, beats through the actor's very pores and out to the audience. It may be far different from the external action, even its opposite. Through inner rhythm a seasoned actor can stand unmoving and silent onstage, yet exude a wrenching internal struggle that makes him appear anything but still. Without saying a word, he is acting.

NOVELIST'S ADAPTATION

Inner rhythm betrays a character's emotions even when she tries to suppress or hide them. Without a sense of a character's unique inner rhythm, the novelist relies on external action to depict feelings in a general way. Gestures and conversation can seem stereotyped, one-dimensional, even false. When an author begins with inner rhythm and works toward the external, each action, facial expression, and spoken word then illuminates the struggle within. Readers *feel* the emotion.

We've all experienced watching an actor who "lived" his part. Every line spoken, every action was so vibrant with emotion that we felt the character's joy and pain. Contrast this to another type of actor we've seen all too often—the one who is wooden in his role. Oh, the appropriate actions are there, and the voice inflection and expressions, but we don't believe any of them. The character is flat. He fails to move us.

What's the difference? *Inner rhythm.*

This same concept applied to our characters' emotions can give a novelist some downright smashing results.

Inner Rhythm and the Portrayal of Emotions

"Rhythm" may seem an unlikely word to apply to emotions. When we hear the word we usually think of music—a song is fast or slow, syncopated or steady. But rhythm doesn't just apply to music; it's all around us, in everything we do. There's the lazy, contented rhythm of lingering in bed on a Saturday morning; the frantic rhythm of dashing for a train; the lulling, hypnotic rhythm of ocean waves. Our bodies respond to certain emotions with rhythm; in tense situations our hearts beat faster, our breaths grow short and ragged. When we stop to think about rhythm in this way, we realize it's not that we are unfamiliar with inner rhythm, but rather we are so familiar with it that we rarely consider its existence. It is as innate and instinctive as breathing. But as novelists, who must constantly study human nature in order to re-create it on paper, we must bring inner rhythm to a conscious level, scrutinize its subtleties, and learn how to employ it for our characters.

I'm not advocating that you'll need to discover the inner rhythm of every character in every scene. But when you've written a scene that seems emotionally flat, or if you're approaching a scene and can't quite figure out specific movements or reactions of your character, inner rhythm can help.

When everything else is said and done—
when characters are well rounded and their
motivation consistent, when setting is
effectively described—look to inner rhythm
to polish the scene.

I once critiqued a novel whose opening scene failed to draw me in to the protagonist's emotions. Yet all other aspects of the scene were well done. The character had been a spy in a foreign city for two years, plotting and planning for the moment that was about to occur. He knew an enemy army was about to burst through the city and overthrow it. At that moment, he would steal the treasures he wanted and flee back to his homeland. The setting was in ancient times, and the novelist had done a wonderful job in describing the unwitting city and its pageantry. And once the action began, it clicked right along. But I could not connect with the character as he lurked in the shadows, anticipating the army's imminent attack. I should have felt his tension, his anxiety, but I didn't.

In reading the scene a second time, I realized what was missing. As this character waited, he displayed very little sign of the *inner rhythm* he would have been experiencing at such a moment. There he was, after two years' meticulous planning, supposedly poised to spring into action. Numerous thoughts of what could go wrong were cycling through his head. Yet he just stood quietly waiting. No sign in his movements of fear, apprehension, the rush of adrenaline. No feel of his muscles tensing, shivering with the knowledge of action to come. And because he didn't exude it I didn't feel it, even though the author informed me, through the character's thoughts of all possible mishaps, that I should.

Let me give you a true-life example of inner rhythm at its most powerful. I witnessed this scene, and to this day it haunts me.

I'd been on my way to the grocery store and was stopped at a long light opposite the high school. Through the passenger window of my car, the figures of a teenage girl and boy caught my eye. Both had their backs to me. The girl was chubby, her blond hair pulled back into a scraggly ponytail. She stood near the curb, her shoulders rounded, leaning forward toward the boy. She was pleading, sobbing; this I knew without seeing her face. Her arms were held away from her sides, palms up, fingers spread. Every muscle in her body vibrated grief; even separated by glass, I *felt* it. The boy was turned away from her, pressed face-first against the school's chainlink fence a mere ten feet away. Yet the sidewalk between them seemed a chasm. His baggy jeans, their crotch halfway to his knees, was topped by a white T-shirt, untucked. His torso was twisted, his feet wide apart. His head was buried in the crook of his left arm, his right arm flung out, fingers curled and whitened around the chain link. The hunch of both shoulders, the odd tilt of his frame, oozed with a mixture of guilt and fear. Whatever the girl was pleading he knew was right, yet he could not grant her request. He could not even bring himself to turn and face her. Self-loathing weighted his bent neck.

I hit a button and my car window slid down. The girl's voice, choked and raw, tumbled around me. *"Pleeease."* The word sounded husky, broken in half. Her shoulders expanded, then fell as she breathed.

The boy wrenched his head toward the right, wiped an eye on his shirt sleeve. "I'm *going!*" His answer was hoarse, defensive.

She sobbed. "Then at least say goodbye to your daughter."

The boy buried his head once more in his arm, pressing further against the wire as if tensed for a fatal bullet.

Then I saw another girl at the edge of this scene. She was tall, willowy, with a baby in her arms, awaiting her cue from the sidelines as these two young parents battled the consequences of one night's choice. The baby looked ruddy-cheeked and already pudgy, a pink bonnet cradling her head. A tiny yet looming presence intended to persuade. Dry-eyed, the girl approached and handed the baby to her mother, then stepped back.

Mother and baby moved toward the boy. At the sound of her footsteps, a groan rattled through his chest.

The stoplight turned green. I drove away.

No words at first. Very little movement. No facial expression, for his back was to me. Yet as soon as I saw this boy, even before rolling down the window to listen, I *felt* his internal struggle. Guilt. Self-loathing. A desire to flee and never look back. I'd never seen this boy before and had no knowledge of the events that had led up to this moment. Yet within seconds, I understood completely.

Why?

Because of his inner rhythm, which displayed itself through unconscious action.

Let's take a closer look at the boy in this scene. We'll call him Jay and the girl Cindy. Here's how I imagine the events preceding this scene. Jay has determined he's leaving town. Maybe his parents are divorced, and he's moving away to live with the other parent—anything to leave his new unwanted responsibility behind. Nothing is going to change his mind. Yet he is not uncaring. Quite the contrary, he does care for Cindy. Perhaps he's even held the baby a few times, and she wound a tiny fist around his finger. She may as well have wound it around his heart. Jay's feelings for Cindy and the baby give rise to a general inner rhythm of affection whenever Jay is around Cindy. Yet the thought of the responsibilities overwhelms him. What about his plans, what about school, his friends? He isn't ready to be a father, that's all there is to it. He *can't* do it, even though he's ridden with guilt over running away.

Now imagine Jay getting out of school this particular afternoon, and Cindy shows up to persuade him to stay, supported by her friend, who carries the baby. At first he freezes at the sight of them. At this point his emotions kick into two distinct and contrasting inner rhythms that quickly drown out the rhythm of his affection for her.

The first rhythm rises from his desire to run. It's a fast and frenetic pace of fear that causes his muscles to tense, his adrenaline to flow. He wishes he could run to some place where he need never face the consequences of his act again, where he could forget the baby even exists.

But he doesn't run because of the second inner rhythm, which rises from guilt. Jay cares enough for Cindy and the baby to know he's doing the wrong thing, and he hates himself for it. The inner rhythm of his guilt is slow, weighty, cumbersome, rendering him almost incapable of movement.

Notice how these two widely diverse inner rhythms affect Jay's choice of action.

The fear and desire to run propel him away from Cindy but only as far as the fence, because his guilt compels him to stay. As a result of the first rhythm, he leans against the chain link, twists his body to the left away from her, buries his head in the crook of that arm. His shoulders hunch with tension; his feet plant firmly into the ground. He's not going anywhere, but his inner rhythm beats, "I'm running; I'm denying." These actions are Jay's way of "burying his head in the sand." Cindy begins pleading for him to turn around. Soon she is sobbing. Her pain increases the guilt within Jay, and this second inner rhythm causes him to react in some amazing ways. He spreads his legs apart. He stretches out his right arm. His fingers clench the chain link. Unconsciously, three-quarters of his body has assumed the position of being spread-eagled before a firing squad or stretched across a torturer's rack. It is the stance of awaiting punishment.

This is what I knew instinctively when I first laid eyes on him.

I certainly didn't analyze. I didn't consciously dissect his every movement and categorize it. That came much later, when I'd had time to pull back from my own emotion and could examine what had so moved me. At the time of the scene I was far too captivated to do anything but *feel*. For on a gut level, from human to human, I sensed this boy's pain.

Now, imagine my preparing to write this scene in a novel. Without an understanding of these inner rhythms and how they would uniquely affect the character of Jay, I probably would not have created the actions described above. I would have thought about Jay's fear and guilt and tried to portray those emotions, to be sure. But they likely would have been depicted through action bordering on stereotype. Perhaps Jay would have walked away from Cindy, hung his head, turned and retraced his steps, said his one line, then walked away again. Inevitably, readers may have *understood* that Jay was feeling afraid and guilty, but they wouldn't have *felt* it.

Hearing Inner Rhythm and Translating It into Action

Two steps are involved in using inner rhythm effectively. First, we need to "hear" the inner rhythm of the character. Second, we must translate the inner rhythm into action that is believable for that particular character. We'll look at two very different techniques for hearing your character's inner rhythm. Regardless of which technique you use, the means for translating the inner rhythm into action is the same.

Technique 1: By involving your body, you can feel the inner rhythm of your character in a tangible way.

In *Building a Character,* Stanislavsky introduced the concept of inner rhythm by asking his students to literally beat on their desks various rhythms of scenes from their own lives, much as one would beat out the rhythm of a song. He asked one student to beat out the rhythm of learning drills in the military. Another student beat out the emotions he felt upon reaching home at the end of the day. For hours they beat out different scenarios from their lives while their colleagues tried to guess what scenes they were tapping. As the students beat these rhythms, an interesting thing happened. They began to feel the emotions of the particular scene building within them, making them relive the moment. Consequently, they were convinced that their classmates would be able to guess what the rhythms stood for. But most of the time the others could not guess. By the end of the long day, the students were all thinking the same thing: This rhythm business didn't work at all. But Stanislavsky set them straight. "I gave you these exercises not for the ones who listened but for you who were doing the beating," he explained. "It is not important whether the others understood you or not. It is far more essential that the rhythm you were conducting spurred your own imaginations to work, suggesting to you certain surrounding circumstances and corresponding emotions."

We, too, can use Stanislavsky's beating-out exercise. To see how this exercise works, let's start with a very simple scenario. Imagine a woman out for a drive on a country road one beautiful afternoon. She's behind a slow-moving farm truck, but she doesn't mind, for she's simply enjoying the sights. In this case, both her inner rhythm and the external rhythm of the scene's environment will be similar—slow and leisurely. Just for the sake of trying it (and because nobody's watching), beat out your version of this rhythm with both hands on a table or desk. If you do this for a minute or two, you'll begin to feel the rhythm within yourself. Notice what this take-your-time rhythm does to your breathing, the way you hold your body.

Now, let's add a dimension. Once again, the woman is behind the same truck on the same country road. But she's feeling anything but leisurely. She is on her way to an interview that could make or break her career. She *cannot* be late. The freeway was backed up due to an accident, so she took the exit for this road hoping to make up for lost time. But it's very curvy, with a double yellow line, and she's frantically looking for a chance to pass the truck.

Of course, you know this hectic inner rhythm will affect the character's external movements as she drives. But let's move beyond stereotyped effects such as gripping the steering wheel or muttering in frustration. What might this character do that is natural yet fresh?

To discover some answers within yourself, try beating out this frantic inner rhythm with your right hand. How fast is the rhythm you're beating? Is it steady or syncopated? What urgency does it contain? How much harder is your hand hitting the surface than in the former leisurely beat?

Now add the original slow rhythm of the external environment with your left hand. What happens? If you're like me, the frenetic pace of the right hand interferes with what the left hand is trying to do. Even though I manage to keep the pace of my left hand slow, the fingers want to flutter between beats. I also notice subtle changes in my entire body. My back tightens, one eye squints a little in concentration. My right shoulder tenses while my left does not. After a while my head begins to nod firmly in time with the left hand, as if helping it along. The soles of my feet press harder into the floor while the heels are raised.

What happens to you?

Whatever reactions you experience can be translated into describing the actions of your character. Understand that *translation* is the key. Otherwise, all your characters will end up portraying your own physical tendencies. This beating-out exercise is merely a way to get your body and emotions involved so that you better understand the situation your character is facing. Once you are "hearing" the inner rhythm, you can blend it with your character's personalized traits and mannerisms, and with his action objectives for the scene, to create action that is believable and full of emotion.

> Inner rhythm + Personalizing + Action objectives = Emotive action

Here's a real-life example of this equation. My eleven-year-old daughter loves to sing. Many times when she's happy or content she'll hum under her breath without even realizing it. Last summer my husband was trying to teach her how to water-ski. She'd finally relented after a few years of refusing because of her fear. As she waited in the water for the boat to rev, we heard her purposefully singing. My husband and I looked at each other and said, "She's nervous." Now, singing is the last thing most people would do when they're nervous, but knowing Amberly, we understood that this was her unique way of trying to calm her nerves.

In this short scene, Amberly's inner rhythm plus her traits and mannerisms were working together with her action objectives to push her into her own unique action. Her initial action objective was: to get up on skis for the first time. But once she got into the water, her inner rhythm changed from resolve to nervousness. This feeling was evidently uncomfortable to her. A new action objective then arose: to deny her nervousness. Amberly's unique, resulting action was to sing.

To recap, here are the steps to take for applying inner rhythm to a character:

1. Beat out the various rhythms of your character in a specific scene. These can include one or more inner rhythms, plus the external rhythm of the scene's environment. Move from the simplest to the most complex. Then try beating two different rhythms at the same time, one with each hand.

2. Note how your body responds while beating the different rhythms. What is each part of your body doing? What are you feeling? Jot down your reactions.

3. Blend your reactions with your character's personalized traits and mannerisms. How would your unique character respond to these reactions? How would these responses combine with the character's action objectives to create emotive action?

With these steps in mind, let's go back to Jay. Try beating out the inner rhythm of his guilt with one hand and his fear/desire to run away with the other. First start with the guilt. Is your rhythm slow and methodical? Or full of pauses? Heavy-handed? Is your palm involved or just your fingers? Then add the fear with the other hand. What are the characteristics of this rhythm? How do the two rhythms affect each other? To carry the exercise even further (and if you're really feeling brave), get up and move around. Stomp out first one rhythm, then the other. What do you feel during each one? What actions might one of your own characters take in Jay's situation?

You can do this exercise for any emotion or feeling. How would you beat out the rhythm of jealousy? Sorrow? Betrayal? Hunger?

Okay, novelists, if you're still with me, we can go on to the second technique for hearing your character's inner rhythm. (I'll bet you're probably glad about now that you're not an actor.) You can sit back down and relax for this one.

Technique 2: Play psychiatrist with your character, questioning him moment by moment through a scene.

Picture yourself as psychiatrist, with your character on the couch. He's under hypnosis, and you want him to tell you in detail every emotion he will feel, and every physical action he'll undertake, when faced with the events of the scene you're about to write. Let's use the encounter between Jay and Cindy as an example.

Jay, you're hanging around on the sidewalk after school and Cindy shows up. What's the first thing you feel?

I want to run away.

Why?

I can't face her. I just want to deny this whole thing ever happened.

How does your body respond?

My heart starts beating really hard. My legs get all tight. My throat gets tight, too.

What else do you feel?

Guilty. I know leaving her is wrong, but I just can't help it. I don't want to be a father!

What does the guilt do to your body?

It makes my feet feel like they weigh a ton. And my chest hurts.

What do you do?

I turn away from her. But it's hard to move, I'm so sick inside. I lean against the fence for support.

She's talking to you, Jay, pleading with you. What do you do next?

I bury my head in my arm. I wish I could block my ears. I just can't stand this! I care for her, but right now I almost hate her for what she's doing to me. My fingers grip the fence tighter and tighter as she keeps talking. I can hardly breathe. My stomach is all upset.

And so on.

There's an interesting twist to this technique. Even though it's not a physical exercise like Technique 1, as you begin to hear your character's inner rhythm, your body still may respond. For example, when I think of Jay's tightened throat, I find myself automatically swallowing. As I imagine his first sight of Cindy, my eyes close in despair, and I feel a sick expression stealing across my face. Even if your body doesn't respond, your mind will begin running with all sorts of ideas for your character's actions. Again, jot down these ideas, then blend them with your character's traits and mannerisms, plus her action objectives, to discover those actions that will innately display her inner rhythm.

After hearing your character's inner rhythm and discovering her subsequent actions through either of the two techniques discussed above, you'll be ready to write a vivid, compelling scene that your readers will *feel*. In the next chapter, we'll talk about specific writing techniques that will help you best present all the emotions and actions you now know of your character. But first, study the following excerpts to better understand the concept of inner rhythm.

 Study Samples

These two scenes show the intensity of inner rhythm in two very different situations. The first scene involves the rhythms of a mob, and the second involves the rhythms of a mother facing the worst situation she could ever face.

FROM

A Tale of Two Cities
by Charles Dickens

Setting: Saint Antoine, an impoverished district of Paris, near the beginning of the French Revolution in 1789. For years the common people's anger has been building against the French aristocracy, who stuff themselves with delicacies and the best things in life while sneering with contempt at the poor, who must scrabble for a mere bit of bread. Wine-shop owners Ernest Defarge and his wife are leaders of the revolutionaries. They and their followers have already swept through Paris, forcing their way into the Bastille and releasing its prisoners. But the mob's anger against individuals who have persecuted them is still not vented. A week has passed since the storming of the Bastille.

Madame Defarge, with her arms folded, sat in the morning light and heat, contemplating the wine-shop and the street. In both, there were several knots of loungers, squalid and miserable, but now with a manifest sense of power enthroned on their distress. The raggedest nightcap, awry on the wretchedest head, had this crooked significance in it: 'I know how hard it has grown for me, the wearer of this, to support life in myself; but do you know how easy it has grown for me, the wearer of this, to destroy life in you?' Every lean bare arm, that had been without work before, had this work always ready for it now, that it could strike. The fingers of the knitting women were vicious, with the experience that they could tear. There was a change in the appearance of Saint Antoine; the image had been hammering into this for hundreds of years, and the last finishing blows had told mightily on the expression.

Madame Defarge sat observing it, with such suppressed approval as was to be desired in the leader of the Saint Antoine women. One of her sisterhood knitted beside her. The short, rather plump wife of a starved grocer, and the mother of two children withal, this lieutenant had already earned the complimentary name of The Vengeance.

'Hark!' said The Vengeance. 'Listen, then! Who comes?'

As if a trail of powder laid from the outermost bound of the Saint Antoine Quarter to the wine-shop door, had been suddenly fired, a fast-spreading murmur came rushing along.

'It is Defarge,' said madame. 'Silence, patriots.'

Defarge came in breathless, pulled off a red cap he wore, and looked round him! 'Listen, everywhere!' said madame again. 'Listen to him!' Defarge stood, panting, against a background of eager eyes and open mouths, formed outside the door; all those within the wine-shop had sprung to their feet.

'Say then, my husband. What is it?'

'News from the other world!'

'How, then?' cried madame, contemptuously. 'The other world?'

'Does everybody here recall old Foulon, who told the famished people that they might eat grass, and who died, and went to Hell?'

'Everybody!' from all throats.

'The news is of him. He is among us!'

'Among us!' from the universal throat again. 'And dead?'

'Not dead! He feared us so much—and with much reason—that he caused himself to be represented as dead, and had a grand, mock-funeral. But they have found him alive, hiding in the country, and have brought him in. I have seen him but now, on his way to the Hotel de Ville, a prisoner. I have said that he had reason to fear us. Say all! Had he reason?'

Wretched old sinner of more than threescore years and ten, if he had never known it yet, he would have known it in his heart of hearts if he could have heard the answering cry.

A moment of profound silence followed. Defarge and his wife looked steadfastly at one another. The Vengeance stooped, and the jar of a drum was heard as she moved it at her feet behind the counter.

'Patriots!' said Defarge, in a determined voice, 'are we ready?'

Instantly Madame Defarge's knife was in her girdle; the drum was beating in the streets, as if it and a drummer had flown together by magic; and The Vengeance, uttering terrific shrieks, and flinging her arms about her head like all the forty Furies at once, was tearing from house to house, rousing the women.

The men were terrible, in the bloody-minded anger with which they looked from windows, caught up what arms they had, and came pouring down into the streets; but, the women were a sight to chill the boldest. From such household occupations as their bare poverty yielded, from their children, from their aged and their sick crouching on the bare ground, famished and naked, they ran out with streaming hair, urging one another, and themselves, to madness with the wildest cries and actions. Villain Foulon taken, my sister! Old Foulon taken, my mother! Miscreant Foulon taken, my daughter! Then, a score of others ran into the midst of these, beating their breasts, tearing their hair, and screaming, Foulon alive! Foulon who told the starving people they might eat grass! Foulon who told my old father that he might eat grass, when I had no bread to give him! Foulon who told my baby it might suck grass, when these breasts were dry with want! O mother of God, this Foulon! O Heaven, our suffering! Hear me, my dead baby and my withered father: I swear on my knees, on these stones, to avenge you on Foulon! Husbands, and brothers, and young men, Give us the blood of Foulon, Give us the body and soul of Foulon, Rip Foulon to pieces, and dig him into the ground, that grass may grow from him! With these cries, numbers of the women, lashed into blind frenzy, whirled about, striking and tearing at their own friends until they dropped into a passionate swoon, and were only saved by the men belonging to them from being trampled under foot.

Nevertheless, not a moment was lost; not a moment! This Foulon was at the Hotel de Ville, and might be loosed. Never, if Saint Antoine knew its own sufferings, insults, and wrongs! Armed men and women flocked out of the Quarter so fast, and drew even these last dregs after them with such a force of suction, that within a quarter of an hour there was not a human creature in Saint Antoine's bosom but a few old crones and the wailing children.

No. They were all by that time choking the Hall of Examination where this old man, ugly and wicked, was, and overflowing into the adjacent open space and streets. The Defarges, husband and wife, The Vengeance, and Jacques Three, were in the first press, and at no great distance from him in the Hall.

'See!' cried madame pointing with her knife. 'See the

old villain bound with ropes. That was well done to tie a
bunch of grass upon his back. Ha, ha! That was well done.
Let him eat it now!' Madame put her knife under her arm,
and clapped her hands as at a play.

The people immediately behind Madame Defarge,
explaining the cause of her satisfaction to those behind
them, and those again explaining to others, and those to
others, the neighbouring streets resounded with the clap-
ping of hands. Similarly, during two or three hours of brawl,
and the winnowing of many bushels of words, Madame
Defarge's frequent expressions of impatience were taken
up, with marvellous quickness, at a distance: the more readily, because certain men who had by some wonderful exercise of agility climbed up the external architecture to look
in from the windows, knew Madame Defarge well, and
acted as a telegraph between her and the crowd outside the
building.

At length the sun rose so high that it struck a kindly ray
as of hope or protection, directly down upon the old prisoner's head. The favour was too much to bear; in an instant
the barrier of dust and chaff that had stood surprisingly long,
went to the winds, and Saint Antoine had got him!

It was known directly, to the furthest confines of the
crowd. Defarge had but sprung over a railing and a table,
and folded the miserable wretch in a deadly embrace—
Madame Defarge had but followed and turned her hand in
one of the ropes with which he was tied—The Vengeance
and Jacques Three were not yet up with them, and the men
at the windows had not yet swooped into the Hall, like
birds of prey from their high perches—when the cry seemed
to go up, all over the city, 'Bring him out! Bring him to the
lamp!'

Down, and up, and head foremost on the steps of the
building; now, on his knees; now, on his feet; now, on his
back; dragged, and struck at, and stifled by the bunches of
grass and straw that were thrust into his face by hundreds of

hands; torn, bruised, panting, bleeding, yet always entreating and beseeching for mercy; now full of vehement agony of action, with a small clear space about him as the people drew one another back that they might see; now, a log of dead wood drawn through a forest of legs; he was hauled to the nearest street corner where one of the fatal lamps swung, and there Madame Defarge let him go—as a cat might have done to a mouse—and silently and composedly looked at him while they made ready, and while he besought her: the women passionately screeching at him all the time, and the men sternly calling out to have him killed with grass in his mouth. Once, he went aloft, and the rope broke, and they caught him, shrieking; twice, he went aloft, and the rope broke, and they caught him shrieking; then, the rope was merciful, and held him, and his head was soon upon a pike, with grass enough in the mouth for all Saint Antoine to dance at the sight of.

Exploration Points

1. What is the contrast between the inner rhythm of the citizens in Saint Antoine and the outer action in the beginning of this scene? How does the inner rhythm position the people to react so quickly to Defarge's announcement?

    The outer rhythm in the beginning of the scene is quiet, slow-paced, with little occurring. Folks are sitting around, observing. Women are knitting. Yet their inner rhythm is fast and furious, and full of vengeance. Their blood is boiling for more action as they pride themselves on their recent victory and keenly watch for their next round of revolutionary fighting. This inner rhythm is displayed in the very way they sit and dress. Dickens infuses even the "raggedest nightcap" or a "lean, bare arm" with a dreadful cockiness. The women knit viciously, "with the experience that they could tear." With deft prose, Dickens shows us that every person in the room is a bomb waiting to explode.

2. As the crowd moves into action, their outer and inner rhythms converge. Here is a moment of surprising emotive action. Some women are so overcome at the mere thought of revenge that they spend themselves in fits before they can take part in fulfilling their long-awaited chance. What types of traits and mannerisms might these women have? How might their action objectives differ from those of the other women?

There are numerous conjectures for this answer. I imagine that these women could possess very opposite traits. Some may have a tendency toward impulsiveness and/or easily displaying emotion. These traits in themselves could lead to their "blind frenzy." Others may usually be very self-contained and viewed as emotionally strong. But a woman such as this, who has kept herself together in spite of her loss of loved ones, may react to the news of Foulon's arrest quite differently. Although, like the other women, her initial action objective may be to kill Foulon, as she's caught up in the fray, another objective could arise: to release the pent-up emotion that she's held within her for so long. As a result, she falls into a "blind frenzy," fighting against her own friends, and so spends herself that she cannot take part in killing Foulon. Dickens's masterful understanding of the inner rhythm of such women lends believability and an even more chilling aura to the scene.

3. The crowd rushes to the Hotel de Ville and sees the old man, tied and helpless. Then more surprising emotive action. They stop. For a long time they mock him, play with him. How has their inner rhythm changed? How does this new rhythm reflect their years of hardship?

Their action objective to kill Foulon has not changed. But their inner rhythm has slowed as a good bit of their energy has been spent in the headlong rush to find him. Again, Dickens shows his masterful understanding of human emotions. Once the revolutionaries know that Foulon—the symbol of the aristocracy, who have caused their impoverishment—is absolutely helpless in their hands, a new action objective arises within them: to revel once again in their long-awaited, sudden place of power. And so they stop their headlong rush to kill in order to mock Foulon at length. They want to see him face the helplessness they've endured for years. He and his peers have mocked them as their loved ones died in wretchedness; now they mock him as he faces an inevitable, wretched death.

Dickens's understanding of this inner rhythm led him to use a simple sun ray as the instigation for their renewed frenzy. The people of Saint Antoine are reveling in Foulon's suddenly "dark" existence. How dare the sun shine on him! The time has come for the sun to shine only on *them*. The merest metaphorical hint of any ray of hope for Foulon is too much for the revolutionaries, and they swarm in for the kill. But even then they want to enjoy it, and they drag the deed out, pouring all of their past humiliation upon Foulon as they make him suffer, as he has made them suffer.

FROM

The Deep End of the Ocean
by Jacquelyn Mitchard

Setting: Chicago, 1985. Three-year-old Ben Cappadora disappears from the lobby of a hotel while his mother, Beth, checks in for her high school reunion. Four and one-half hours later, the little boy is still missing. Detective Supervisor Candy Bliss has been called to the scene to help find him. In this scene, Candy is questioning a distraught and still disbelieving Beth and Beth's seven-year-old son, Vincent, who was supposed to have been watching his little brother when Ben disappeared. Pat is Ben and Vincent's father.

[Candy Bliss] got up and settled herself on the luggage trolley, where Vincent cringed. "You wanta help the cops, Vincent? We got a lost brother here." Vincent stared around her, at Beth. Beth nodded faintly. "First, I want you to point for me in which direction Ben walked away."

Vincent sat back down on the luggage trolley and coiled back against the wall beside the elevator, hiding his eyes with uncharacteristic reluctance, until Beth walked over and settled him on her lap. Then he buried his face against Beth's midriff and violently shook his head. Beth eased him up and brushed the sweaty hair off his forehead.

"You can help find Ben. Old fuzzhead Ben needs you," she told him. Vince squeezed his eyes closed; like her, Beth thought, he wanted to shrink to a dot.

"He's shrinking," she told Candy Bliss, who blinked once, quickly, and then looked away.

"Come on, buddy," the detective urged Vincent. "Show me where your brother went."

Vincent stuck out one limp and skinny arm and pointed toward the center of the room.

If Ben had toddled—Beth caught herself using the word, making Ben tinier, more babylike than he really was—off in that direction, he would have come gradually closer and closer to Beth.

He had been trying to come to Beth.

"Did you poke him?" Beth asked Vincent, suddenly, ferociously.

"No, I didn't touch him one single time!"

"Was he frightened? Did he want me?"

"No—Ellen. He wanted me to get Aunt Ellen. He said he was peeing his pants."

Beth loosed her arms from around Vincent; he flopped forward. She clawed her face again—Ben helpless, Ben embarrassed and looking for a trusted grownup, any of his "safe grownups," to help him use the bathroom. Had he seen her? Had he called? Had he tried to find a washroom on his own? Beth stood up, reeled, sat down heavily on the luggage trolley.

"I can think of better places to fall than that thing," Bliss said. "Why don't we get you on a couch?"

Lie down, Beth thought. It was the suggestion you made

all the time in disasters, to people waiting to hear about the survivors of downed aircraft, to the stranded, to those in hospital emergency rooms awaiting the results of doomed surgeries. Have coffee. Lie down. Try to eat something. She had said it herself, to Pat's cousin (Jill's mother, Rachelle) last year, when Jill, then a freshman, had been hit by a car on her bike and had a leg broken in three places. Rachelle had listened; she lay down and slept.

Beth supposed she should lie down; her throat kept filling with nastiness and her stomach roiled. But if she lay down, she wanted to explain to Candy Bliss, who was holding out her hand, it would be deserting Ben. Did Detective Bliss think Ben was lying down? If Beth ate, would he eat? She should not do anything Ben couldn't do or was being prevented from doing. Was he crying? Or wedged in a dangerous and airless place? If she lay down, if she rested, wouldn't Ben feel her relaxing, think she had decided to suspend her scramble toward him, the concentrated thrust of everything in her that she held out to him like a life preserver? Would he relax then, turn in sorrow toward a bad fate, because his mama had let him down?

Surely this woman would understand how urgently Beth needed to remain upright.

She smiled brightly at Candy Bliss and said, "He's not dead."

"No, of course not, Beth."

"If he were dead, I could tell. A mother could tell."

"That's what they say."

"It's true, though. They talk to you with their minds, your kids. You wake up before they wake up—not because you hear them cry; you hear them getting ready to cry." Beth had never thought about the sinister extension of that link before—that if Ben were now being tortured or suffocating, she would feel a searing pain in her, perhaps in her belly, her throat. She was, instantly, entirely sure of this; there would be a physical alert, a signal at the cellular level. She strained up on the end of her spine, to raise her aerial, her sensors. She felt nothing, smelled and heard nothing, not even a whisper of breathed air past her ear.

And then Pat came up out of the basement of the hotel, yelling, "Where's your phone? I have to call my father and mother, and my cousin, my sisters!"

No, Beth thought, not them all. And yet, perhaps, if they came—and then went—she could follow her feelers, delicate feelers deranged by all this light and sound, into the night, clear. She could rise up from this pond bottom, from where she watched Pat, and let Ben pull her to him. Pull his mother to him with the gravitational force of their bond.

It was seven p.m.

She watched as Vincent soundlessly, furiously threw himself on Pat—and Pat had sufficient presence of will to show love for Vincent even now, to bury his face in Vincent's neck. "Don't worry, Vincenzo," he said, "Papa will find Ben."

Mama, Beth thought. Mama will find Ben. Maybe.

She leaned forward, delicately and slowly, over the edge of the luggage trolley, and vomited on the tile floor in front of the elevator.

Exploration Points

1. What are the various inner rhythms Beth is feeling in this scene?

   This is a scene of many inner rhythms that fight each other. The dreadful, enervating rhythm of utter fear and shock. The quickened, staccato rhythm of wanting to *do* something—of seeking helpful action that refuses to be found. The fluttering rhythm of helplessness. The heavy, firm rhythm of denial. The penetrating rhythm of guilt. The cautious rhythm of worry and protectiveness for Vincent. The determined rhythm of willing herself to stay in control.

2. What specific (and sometimes surprising) emotive actions do these inner rhythms cause Beth to take?

   She is tender toward Vincent until her guilt and fear overwhelm her. As a result, she lashes out at him. Then she removes her protective arms from him to claw at herself. Her desire to do something drives her to her feet, but her helplessness forces her back down. In turn, her desire for action causes her to refuse to lie down. In one moment her fear for Ben becomes so acute that it immediately pushes her into denial, and she "smiles brightly" as she declares he's not dead. Her shock leads her to throw up, but even then, her determination to avoid panic makes her lean over "delicately and slowly."

3. Review and edit a scene you've written in which inner rhythm could be used to propel your characters to emotive action. How will these rhythms affect your characters in subsequent scenes?

Moving On

In the last five chapters we have discussed numerous techniques to help you discover new truths about your character. We've come all the way from personalizing to inner rhythm. You are poised to write about your character in ways you never have before. Now, how to best present all that knowledge—all those truths about your character—on paper? We turn to some specific writing techniques to help you write a scene in the most compelling way possible. These are techniques adapted from the Method acting concepts of Secret #6: Restraint and Control.

Restraint and Control

ACTOR'S TECHNIQUE:

As a painter needs a clean, white canvas upon which to create a picture, an actor needs a body that is cleared of her own natural gestures so she may discover movements that are true to the character. Superfluous movements cause two problems: they divert energy away from gestures that are appropriate, and they weaken characterization by blurring the overall performance. To avoid such movements, an actor must practice *restraint and control*.

NOVELIST'S ADAPTATION:

An actor creates a character through choice of movements; a novelist creates a character through choice of words. If a scene is weak or moves too slowly, it may be the result of superfluous or poorly chosen words—words that blur the focus of the scene and slow the pace. Through *restraint and control* a novelist learns how to use the best words to flesh out characters, create an aura, and move the scene forward.

The Blending of Technique and Characterization

Consider for a moment the challenge our acting cousins face. For months an actor has studied her part, learned her lines. She's ready to live and breathe her character. Then comes that moment of stepping onto the stage to perform. The wood floor suddenly seems so vast, the curtains so high. The actor's limbs tense, her mouth goes dry, and her mind blanks. She speaks a line, makes a motion, and feels her own mannerisms threatening to surface, even after all her studying of the role.

We could say this nervous actor has to "pull herself together." But actually, to effectively portray all the characterization brimming within her, she must allow herself to "split" into two personas. The first is her character, living out her life on the stage. The Method actor must *become* that character—feeling her emotions, desires, joys, and disappointments. This, in fact, is the essence of Method acting. The second persona is herself, the actor, the technique-watcher. This persona almost stands back as a separate entity, judging her technical performance. Is she speaking her lines loudly enough? Has she turned her back to the stage? Is she remembering the blocking of the scene?

The Method actor will tell you this "splitting" is the moment of truth. She must carry each persona equally well. All the characterization in the world will amount to little if the audience can't hear her lines, see her expressions. On the contrary, all the theatrical techniques in the world—the most resonant voice, the most perfectly memorized lines—will seem vain and empty without the soul of a character beneath them.

Glad you're not an actor? All right, allow yourself a quick sigh of relief. Then remember the challenge *you* face.

The blank page.

Like the actor, you've done your homework. You know your characters. You've plotted your story; or at least, you know your story's main events. If you're like me, you may have movies of scenes and action and emotions running through your head. But now, like the actor, you must "split" into two personas. The first one cries and laughs and defies and trembles with your characters. The second sits before the blank page, sorting through writing techniques, asking questions such as: How do I make my readers see the movie in my head? How do I find just the right words to capture the aura, the emotions, of a scene that tumble and swirl through my mind?

In the last five chapters we've discussed numerous secrets to help the first persona. Now, like the actor, we face our moment of truth. The best personalizing, the deepest understanding of our characters' action objectives, subtexted dialogue, colored passions, and inner rhythm, will all be for naught unless we can find the right words to make our readers *feel* with our characters.

We're not going to talk here about the most basic elements of writing, even though they're certainly important. If you've stayed with me this far, you deserve a deeper discussion than one focusing on grammar, punctuation, and active versus passive verbs. We'll focus instead on two writing techniques—our unique adaptation of the actor's concepts of restraint and control. These are the techniques of *sentence rhythm* and *compression*.

Sentence Rhythm

Just as inner rhythm focuses on the inner "beat" of a character, the technique of sentence rhythm, as its name implies, focuses on the rhythm or "beat" of your sentences. You may not tend to think of your sentences as having rhythm, but they certainly do. And different sentence rhythms create different feelings, as in music. A fast beat in a song makes you want to dance; a slow, easy beat makes you want to sway. Once you understand how sentence rhythm works, you can use it to help create the desired aura of a scene.

> The rhythm of your sentences should match the "beat" of action in your scene.

Most of the time (we'll cover an exception shortly), long sentences will lull the reader, while short, choppy, or even incomplete sentences are more jarring. If your character is daydreaming by a babbling brook, long sentences are fine. Their very "beat" gives the sense of peace and tranquility that ideally complements the setting. But in times of suspense or action, your sentences should beat the rhythm that the character feels as he faces danger. This rhythm is staccato, choppy. It carries a sense of fear, of the unexpected.

Not that readers understand this concept on a conscious level, mind you. But unconsciously, they will feel it. If a reader must wade through long sentences when the scene's action is supposed to quicken her heartbeat, she won't feel the aura that you're trying to create. Why? Because the lulling rhythm she "hears" in her head as she reads your sentences will fight your intended rhythm of danger.

> For action or suspense, shorten your
> sentences.

If your scene begins quietly or perhaps with narrative, then action starts, switch to shorter sentences at that point. Here and there you might use only phrases. In very intense action, as in life-and-death danger sequences, you can even use one-word sentences.

Here's an example from my novel *Color the Sidewalk for Me*, of a quiet scene hitting sudden action. The first two paragraphs show the character's hesitant and thought-filled walk through woods. The third paragraph—only one sentence—transitions into the action. Note how sentences in the following paragraphs shorten when the action begins. Even the longer sentences are divided into shorter phrases of individual action. The whole feel becomes choppy, more intense, like the sudden quickening of the character's heartbeat.

A few moments later, I'd entered the grove, relative coolness surrounding me. I paused to wipe sweat from my face. Following the weaving path, I listened for Danny but heard only the sound of my own footsteps. *He's not coming,* I taunted myself, *he doesn't want me*. Leaning against the last tree, I berated my impetuousness. What now? I certainly couldn't appear on Danny's front lawn. Once he saw me, there would be no way to explain myself, no way to slip gracefully from the scruffy grass and the memory of his hand grasping mine. I was no more than a hundred feet from his house. I could almost feel him.

I prayed for him to appear but knew I'd already waited too long. I needed to get back to Kevy. My chest sank. Turning to retrace my steps, I tossed a strand of hair from my face, telling myself it didn't matter; I didn't need Danny Cander anyway. Who did he think he was, trying to hurt me? I emerged from the trees, blinking in the sunlight, repeating to myself that I didn't need Danny, I did *not*.

Then the sound wafted from Danny's house, a muffled stridence through the grove.

I halted, skin tingling. Cocked my head. There it was again. A man argued vehemently. A woman's voice pleaded. I held my breath. The pleading escalated, then abruptly stopped.

Silence.

My eyes danced across the field as I waited, muscles tense.

The woman screamed. My heart revved, thudded against my chest . . .

As this scene illustrates, sentence rhythm depends on more than just the length of your sentences. There are no absolute rules (novelists, as a rule, hate rules!), but these additional guidelines will help you create the rhythm you seek.

1. Past participles (past-tense verbs ending in "ing") are best used in quiet, easy-rhythm scenes. When action or suspense begins, use regular past-tense verbs.

   Note the number of past-participle verbs in the first two paragraphs above—*surrounding, following, leaning, blinking, repeating.*

These verbs have the sense of continuation, an action that takes place over time. Because of this sense, they tend to convey a take-it-easy sort of rhythm. Regular past-tense verbs convey a sense of immediacy, of sudden action. For example, once the action starts in the paragraphs above, we see verbs such as *halted, cocked, argued, pleaded, screamed, revved, thudded*.

2. Complex sentences work better in quiet rhythm; simple sentences work better for action.

   This guideline is true for a number of reasons. The first is obvious—complex sentences are by definition longer than simple sentences. Second, complex sentences tend to use participial phrases. Example: *Following the weaving path, I listened for Danny . . .* Or: *Leaning against the last tree, I berated my impetuousness.* Third, complex sentences often make the reader wade through words before reaching the subject and main verb (as in the two example sentences above). In action or suspense sequences, the main verb is the most important word of the sentence. You want to give it prominence, not bury it.

3. In general, the higher the action level, the shorter your sentences should be.

   Shortening your sentences into incomplete phrases gives off the beat of extreme action or fear. A one-word sentence really can pack a punch. Of course, not every sentence can be very short. But you can divide those that are longer into phrases, each carrying its own sense of immediate action. Example: *The pleading escalated, then abruptly stopped.*

4. In high action sequences, such as fight scenes, divide the action and reaction into separate sentences or short phrases within the same sentence.

   The rhythm of fight scenes is rapid-fire, one action leading to another and another. You want your readers to feel the punches, hear the beat of fear. Every action should be definite and strong. The best way to show this strength is to keep each action distinctive, in a unit of its own. For example, consider this chase sequence on a flight of stairs, first without employing sentence rhythm:

Throwing out her fist, she punched him in the eye. Growling in pain, he threw himself on top of her. She was screaming as he pinned her arms and legs. She strained to free herself, lunging up to bite him. He started jerking backwards, and his movements made them slide down a stair.

The beat of these sentences is simply too languid for the rhythm of the scene. Now consider the scene using sentence rhythm as it appears in my novel *Eyes of Elisha*, noting in particular the separation of each action:

Her right fist caught him in the eye. He growled in pain, then threw himself on top of her. She screamed. He pinned her arms, her legs. She strained to free herself, lunged up to bite him. He jerked backwards. They slid down one stair. She tried to scream again. He slapped a palm over her mouth, his breath hot on her face.

So, as you can see, short sentences = action. Most of the time.

There is one important exception. This exception involves scenes that contain action so intense that it moves into chaos. In the scene examples above, we could delineate each action. They were sequential in nature. But in scenes of utter chaos, many things are happening at once. The character or characters are so bombarded by stimuli that they don't have time to react to individual pieces of action. How do you best convey this rhythm?

> For the "beat" of chaos, use long, strung-together sentences to convey continuous, confusing action.

In writing scenes of chaos, you can throw out all four of the guidelines listed above. Create complex sentences, use past participles even write run-on sentences—do anything you must in order for your sentences to beat the rhythm of chaos and confusion.

The study sample from Dickens's A *Tale of Two Cities* that is included in the chapter on inner rhythm contains an excellent example of sentence rhythm that matches the beat of chaos breaking out in a mob. The revolutionaries have cornered their old foe, Foulon, and long moments of tension follow in which they confront and watch him. Then, suddenly, the crowd lunges and chaos erupts as they lynch him:

> Down, and up, and head foremost on the steps of the building; now, on his knees; now, on his feet; now, on his back; dragged, and struck at, and stifled by the bunches of grass and straw that were thrust into his face by hundreds of hands; torn, bruised, panting, bleeding, yet always entreating and beseeching for mercy; now full of vehement agony of action, with a small clear space about him as the people drew one another back that they might see; now, a log of dead wood drawn through a forest of legs; he was hauled to the nearest street corner where one of the fatal lamps swung, and there Madame Defarge let him go—as a cat might have done to a mouse—and silently and composedly looked at him while they made ready, and while he besought her: the women passionately screeching at him all the time, and the men sternly calling out to have him killed with grass in his mouth. Once, he went aloft, and the rope broke, and they caught him, shrieking; twice, he went aloft, and the rope broke, and they caught him shrieking; then, the rope was merciful, and held him, and his head was soon upon a pike, with grass enough in the mouth for all Saint Antoine to dance at the sight of.

Note that the entire paragraph is only two sentences. And the paragraph uses many participles. The resulting effect is the rhythm of perpetual, chaotic motion and confusion.

One more important thing to note about sentence rhythm. So

far, we have focused on the rhythm of *outer* action within a scene. But after studying Secret #5, we know that the *inner* rhythm of a character is just as important. So how do you know which rhythm your sentences should match?

> Sentence rhythm should match your character's inner rhythm when this inner rhythm—rather than external action—is the beat that carries the scene.

Let's go back to that character sitting by the babbling brook. An easy, mellow sentence rhythm is fine as long as he's merely relaxing. But what if his insides are churning? What if he's wrestling with the biggest decision of his entire life? Since you want the reader to hear the beat that most affects your character, you should focus on this inner rhythm. Are his thoughts sequential, distinct? Use the sentence rhythm for action. Are his thoughts completely convoluted and tangled? Then the sentence rhythm of chaos may work best.

In some scenes you can even go back and forth between the inner rhythm of your character and the outer action, changing the rhythm of your sentences accordingly. This changing beat heightens each of the rhythms and their contrast to each other.

Once you understand sentence rhythm, you face the next challenge: how to choose the best words possible to convey all the action of a scene. For help with word choice, we turn now to our second writing technique, compression.

Compression

In a nutshell, "compression" means finding verbs, adjectives, and nouns that are packed with meaning. When your writing is effectively compressed, two results occur: (1) your narrative and action will be more vivid, and (2) you'll use fewer words. Pardon the analogy, but imagine a large bag filled with trash compared with a similar bag in a trash compactor. The latter packs in two to three times as much trash. And as a result, you'll use fewer bags.

We often use the terms "lean" or "tight" writing to refer to the elimination of unnecessary words. Compression is much more than lean writing. I've seen writing that's very lean but also lacking in vividness. Sometimes editing for the pure sake of "leanness" can result in writing that reminds me of a room filled with nothing but Scandinavian furniture. There's nothing wrong with Scandinavian furniture, mind you. It boasts clean lines and is very functional. Still, by itself it's rather boring. I'd want to add a few pictures, a green plant here and there, a knickknack or two. *Now* you've got a room with some personality.

Here's a more specific look at how compression works.

> Vividness springs from effective word choice.

Vividness can encompass both individual words and phrases. Writing vividly means writing in a way that creates a picture in your reader's mind. In action scenes, this picture often is a specific movement or facial expression. In narrative passages this picture helps your reader grasp a certain truth about your character.

Just as with sentence rhythm, compression requires careful attention to verbs, especially during action scenes. You want to find those verbs with the most "bang for the buck." The key is to use the most specific verb possible. Many verbs are just too general to be very descriptive. These include verbs such as stand, look, see, walk, move, talk, sit, and so on. If your character is sitting, is she slouching? Slumping? Perching? Notice how these verbs connote the character's *attitude* as she sits. The first gives the impression of laziness or perhaps defiance; the second shows despondence; the third connotes a high level of energy. In the same way, if your character is looking at someone or something, *how* is she looking? How is she walking, moving, standing? Sometimes these questions are answered by adding an adverb. But we know how easy it is to fall into "-ly" writing. Adverbs are necessary now and then. But if you can replace a general verb and its adverb with one specific verb, do it.

For narrative passages or description, in addition to finding the most specific verb, pay attention to the adjectives and nouns you choose. Look for unusual ways to express your thoughts. Sometimes a metaphor or simile can release a whole aura of meaning that would otherwise need two or three sentences of explanation. Nature and everyday life are your best sources for discovering these unique descriptions. Pay attention to the world around you. Notice how wind ruffles water or moves over a wheat field. How a cat stalks its prey. Hear the click of knitting needles, the crackle of a fire. Note how mist clings to your hair on a foggy day, how your breath hangs in a vapor in the cold. Any one of these natural occurrences releases a vivid mental picture that can be used in description.

The use of vivid verbs and descriptive phrases naturally gives way to the second benefit of compression:

> Vividness leads to the elimination of excess words.

Sometimes just one vivid word can negate the need for an entire "telling" sentence or even a paragraph. We've all heard the (in)famous piece of writing advice, "Show, don't tell." Still, we fall into the "telling" trap all too often, merely because it is so easy. The danger of too much "telling" writing is twofold. First, there is absolutely nothing captivating about it. And second, all the excess words will cause your story to drag.

Remember that vivid writing, particularly with regard to verbs, requires specificity. When you've hit on that just-right compressed word or phrase, you'll no longer need general "telling" description. You can cut long phrases and sentences merely designed to explain.

To see how compression can lead to vividness and excess word elimination, let's take a "before and after" look at the opening of my true crime book, *A Question of Innocence:*

> Sharri Moore had read her daughter's diaries more times than she could remember. She had to, Sharri rationalized as she looked at Serena's blue-flowered journal lying on the desk. Sometimes she found important things in the diaries. A lot of the entries were just teenage stuff—about girls who'd been kind to Serena only to be mad at her the next day. Serena would write about these girls with anger and confused betrayal. Other entries were about daydreams or hoped-for things. But sometimes the entries showed aspects of Serena that she would never reveal. Sharri considered these entries nuggets of gold.

The same passage as it was published, using compression:

> When it came to her daughter's diary, Sharri Moore was a snoop. And with good reason, she thought, eyeing Serena's blue-flowered journal as it lay on the desk. Buried among the fantasies, the teenage yearnings, the diatribes against snotty schoolgirls who dangled their friendship like candy beyond a baby's reach, lay occasional nuggets of gold. Glints of the real Serena.

Note how specific words and phrases add vividness in the second version.

1. The explanation that Sharri "had read her daughter's diary more times than she could remember" is now summarized by the word "snoop." This one noun connotes not only the tendency to peek into others' affairs, but to do it consciously and consistently.

2. "Looked" becomes "eyeing," a more intense verb.

3. Two general "telling" sentences are no longer needed: "Sometimes she found important things in the diaries" and "A lot of the entries were just teenage stuff."

4. "Daydreams" and "hoped-for things" become the stronger words "fantasies" and "teenage yearnings." The sentences about other girls and Serena's reaction to them now use vivid words such as "diatribes," "snotty," and "dangled friendship." The simile "like candy beyond a baby's reach" conjures a mental picture of how tantalizing these fickle friendships were to Serena.

5. The metaphor of buried gold amid uninteresting diary entries is a vivid portrayal of just how much Sharri treasured these bits of information.

Compression requires ruthless editing. And learning it takes time and practice. Fact is, true compression relies on all the other techniques we have discussed so far. If you have personalized your character and know her inner values, traits, and mannerisms, you are better equipped to find the most vivid words to describe her thoughts and actions. When you understand your character's action objectives in a scene and can feel her reaction to conflict, you'll be able to write her emotions with compression. Effective subtexting will save you many excess words, compressing meaning into the dialogue itself. Coloring the passions of your character can lead you to vivid words and unique descriptive phrases, as will your understanding of your character's inner rhythm in a given scene.

Our study samples show how both compression and sentence rhythm can combine with these other techniques to create memorable, compelling scenes.

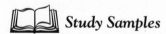 **Study Samples**

Each of these two scenes demonstrates one of our adaptations of restraint and control. The first scene shows the power of compression through vivid word choice. Note the use of compression in describing both the outer scene and the character's emotions. The second scene is a compelling example of sentence rhythm that matches the inner rhythm of a character, which is rapid and syncopated while the outer action remains quiet. The author plays up the inner rhythm by using short sentences and repetition for amazing effect.

FROM

Anna Karenina
by Leo Tolstoy

Setting: Russia, 1870s. Thirty-two-year-old Konstantin Dmitrievitch Levin is in love with the charming young Kitty Shtcherbatsky, whom he has known since childhood. Levin plans to propose marriage to Kitty but has placed her on such a pedestal that he is not sure she will view him as acceptable, even though their families enjoy equal social status. In this scene he seeks her out, hoping to make his proposal.

At four o'clock, conscious of his throbbing heart, Levin stepped out of a hired sledge at the Zoological Gardens, and turned along the path to the frozen mounds and the skating-ground, knowing that he would certainly find her there, as he had seen the Shtcherbatskys' carriage at the entrance.

It was a bright, frosty day. Rows of carriages, sledges, drivers, and policemen were standing in the approach. Crowds of well-dressed people, with hats bright in the sun, swarmed about the entrance and along the well-swept little paths between the houses adorned with carving in the Russian style. The old curly birches of the gardens, all their twigs laden with snow, looked as though freshly decked in sacred vestments.

He walked along the path towards the skating-ground, and kept saying to himself—"You mustn't be excited, you must be calm. What's the matter with you? What do you want? Be quiet, stupid," he conjured his heart. And the more he tried to compose himself, the more breathless he found himself. An acquaintance met him and called him by his name, but Levin did not even recognize him. He went towards the mounds, whence came the clank of the chains of sledges as they slipped down or were dragged up, the rumble of the sliding sledges, and the sounds of merry voices. He walked on a few steps, and the skating-ground lay open before his eyes, and at once, amidst all the skaters, he knew her.

He knew she was there by the rapture and the terror that seized on his heart. She was standing talking to a lady at the opposite end of the ground. There was apparently nothing striking either in her dress or her attitude. But for Levin she was as easy to find in that crowd as a rose among nettles. Everything was made bright by her. She was the smile that shed light on all round her. "Is it possible I can go over there on the ice, go up to her?" he thought. The place where she stood seemed to him a holy shrine, unapproachable, and there was one moment when he was almost retreating, so overwhelmed was he with terror. He had to make an effort to master himself, and to remind himself that people of all sorts were moving about her, and that he too might come there to skate. He walked down, for a long time avoiding looking at her as at the sun, but seeing her, as one does the sun, without looking.

Exploration Points

1. What vivid verbs does Tolstoy use to describe Levin's emotions and actions? How do they help set the tone for the scene?

   Throbbing. Swarmed. Conjured. Slipped down and dragged up. Seized. These words help set the tone by raising the actions of Levin and everyone involved in the scene to greater heights. As a result, the scene is fraught with gravity; it carries the sense of major import. And indeed, this is just how Levin views this moment in time as he pursues his action objective.

2. What similes and metaphors does Tolstoy employ, and how do they add to his vivid descriptions? Note especially the phrase "as

though freshly decked in sacred vestments." Why do you think Tolstoy chose to use this particular simile?

Tolstoy uses certain descriptions to show us how Levin's mind is completely filled with this young woman, and how overwhelmed he is by the thought of proposing to her. The birches "freshly decked in sacred vestments" lend the image of a priest conducting a religious ceremony, such as a wedding. Naturally, a wedding would be in Levin's thoughts. Tolstoy finds numerous ways to tell us how much Kitty stands out in the crowd as far as Levin is concerned. First Kitty is likened to a "rose among nettles." Then she is likened to the sun. "Everything is made bright by her. She was the smile that shed light on all round her." At the end of the example, she is so radiant that Levin sees her even without looking at her, "as one does the sun, without looking." We also see the depth of Levin's intimidation in approaching Kitty as he calls the very place in which she is standing "a holy shrine, unapproachable."

3. Rewrite one or two of your own scenes, using compression. See how many vivid verbs and nouns you can find to improve the scene, while using fewer words overall.

FROM

Passing by Samaria
by Sharon Ewell Foster

Setting: Chicago, 1919. Pearl, an African-American, is walking by himself, just as a race riot is breaking out across the city.

Pearl whistled in the growing darkness. Usually it was the time he felt most comfortable. Darkness was his friend. It made the shapes of the day a little less certain. Darkness blurred the lines between buildings, between people. It hid the borders. Darkness covered what appeared harsh, even filthy during the day. It hid all the unswept corners, all the smudges. It made what was ugly in the daylight beautiful or at least palatable.

Thank God for the darkness, Pearl lifted his hands in praise and mocked Deac, then laughed to himself. He usually enjoyed the darkened journey from the boardinghouse where the Pullman porters lodged to the Stroll.

The laugh, his smile, didn't linger. The air was too quiet, too still. None of the usual sounds. Pearl strained to hear what was missing. His efforts only returned the sound of his feet, loud on the pavement. Worry knocked at his heart, but Pearl shook the shoulders of his outer man and walked on, though he did try to soften the sound of his shoes striking the pavement.

Click, click. Click, click. The second and fourth beats the strongest. *Click*, click, *click*, click. Heels on cobblestones. Pearl's mind went to the rhythm. He began to intentionally accentuate different beats. Click, *click*, click, *click*. Click, click, click, *click*. On his way to get the girl; she would be a diversion on his way to Miami. When he got tired of her . . . that was her problem. Click, click, *click*, *click*.

Still, the uneasiness would not leave. Felt like something on his back. *Click*, *click*, click, click. Like something crawling up his back onto the nape of his neck. He brushed behind his head at nothing, stopped, looked around discomfited.

Stupid, just stupid. The old man. Just letting that old man spook me.

Click, click, *click*, click. Pearl stopped and looked back, then swore at himself. *Click*, click, *click*, click. Nothing else besides his shoes.

I ain't scared of nothing. An invisible freight train rushed past his ears. Sweat soaked his collar. Pant, pant, panting for no reason. He was panting. Looking over his shoulder.

Old fool, old fool. I'm not gone listen to that old fool no more. Won't let him plant that hoodoo in me no more.

Click, click—

Run.

Pearl stopped, looked around. What was that? Almost like a voice, a presence, yelling. The something was crawling up the back of his neck.

"Spooked," he said out loud to himself. "Spooked by an old spook." He tried to laugh off what was chasing him.

Run!

It was like the presence he felt when his mother prayed. When Deac prayed . . .

Click, click, *click,* click.

He stopped to listen. Silence, almost too silent. Like tornado weather.

Some things were the same though. The heat. Thick Chicago nighttime heat and the packing-house smell, a thick foul odor you could slice like hog's head cheese. Something they did in the packing house, some process with the slaughtered animals that made that smell. That smell hung in the summer air. Some things you could count on, most of them bad.

Still something, something just . . . He stopped again to hear.

Now, some sound. Some sound far away rolled to him, fractured in the air, in the smell. From the corner of his eye, he saw it folding in on itself. A ball like in the funnies, like in a cat fight. An arm here, a foot there. Like a blur. Like a ball rolling toward him. Angry men. White men. A mob.

Run now. While another voice, the voice he heard most often in his head now mocked, *Too late.*

Pearl stood still, frozen, and watched the writhing mass move toward him. There now, a face, an angry mouth, two, three, twelve.

Too late now, the other voice mocked louder. *Too late to run now.*

Exploration Points

1. What are the differing, changing beats within Pearl? How does the author use sentence rhythm to convey them?

   This scene is so effective because Foster uses shorter and shorter sentences as Pearl's fear grows, until finally the scene turns on one word.

   When the scene opens, Pearl is at ease, happy, comfortable. The sentences flow in an easy rhythm. As soon as Pearl detects that something is the matter (third paragraph), the sentences become a string of short phrases, and we begin to hear a distinct rhythm: "The air was too quiet, too still." Pearl becomes fearful. Suddenly, sounds he would never notice, like the sound of his shoes on the pavement, become overly loud. He hears the shoes in sets of four: "*Click, click, click, click,*" and the rhythm frightens him more. He forces his mind to other thoughts, and the sentences lengthen for a moment. Nevertheless, they echo the rhythm of his mounting fear by using repetition: "On his way to get the girl; she would be a diversion on his way to Miami." Then, in spite of himself, Pearl focuses again on his shoes: "Click, click, *click, click.*" Next his thoughts shorten into a rhythm of trios: "Stupid, just stupid. The old man." Then Pearl's breathing echoes the rhythm of his shoes, now in twos: "Pant, pant" and "*Click, click.*" And his thoughts echo the same terrifying dual rhythm: "*Old fool, old fool.*" Finally the rhythm shortens to one word: "*Run.*" At this point, we can almost hear Pearl's heart stop as it skips a beat.

2. Toward the end of this scene, the outer action evolves into chaos. What techniques are used to convey the sense of mass confusion?

   First, Foster uses longer sentences: "Thick Chicago nighttime heat and the packing-house smell, a thick, foul odor you could slice like hog's head cheese." Then the chaos is portrayed in an unusual way—through a string of phrases as Pearl, slow to catch on, seems to take in one piece of data at a time: "An arm here, a foot there. Like a blur. Like a ball rolling toward him. Angry men. White men. A mob." We can almost feel the mob envelop Pearl as we read the last rhythmic sentences: "*Too late now*, the other voice mocked louder. *Too late to run now.*"

3. Edit one of your own scenes, using sentence rhythm to convey either the character's inner rhythm or the outer action.

Moving On

All of the techniques we have discussed so far depend upon one important requirement: your ability to connect with your character's emotions. But what if your character must endure or do something that you've never personally experienced? How do you find the inner rhythm, the action objectives, the passions of this character?

To discover how you can create any character, no matter how foreign he or she might seem, let's look to our final Secret, Emotion Memory.

Emotion Memory

ACTOR'S TECHNIQUE:

In bringing forth the emotions of a character, a Method actor relies on his own *emotion memory* to re-create within himself all the sensations and feelings appropriate to his role at the moment. Emotion memory is rooted in the actor's past experiences and can be evoked through such things as a smell, a picture, or a thought. Other times it is more slowly and purposefully recaptured through retelling of a certain past experience.

NOVELIST'S ADAPTATION:

An author carries within himself the seed for every emotion and desire he may create within a character, no matter how foreign that desire may seem to him on the surface. When an author learns how to tap into his emotion memory, he will release himself from every "I-can't-write-that" fear. The world lies at his feet.

Time to get personal.

Up to this point, we've focused on your character. By now you have a clear understanding of how important it is to know your character from the inside out. We've discovered who he is—his inner values, traits, and mannerisms. We've discussed his action objectives, his inner rhythm, his motivations for subtexting, the widely varied colors of his passions. Now we're going to talk about you.

Like it or not, the truth is this: your character's emotions begin with you. You are the well from which every passion of your character—every tremble and smile and tear and jealousy—will be drawn.

Personal Experience as the Basis for Characters' Emotions

As a novelist, you are much further removed from your audience than an actor. An actor displays his or her emotions directly in front of an audience, who can see the movements and facial expressions, hear the tones of voice. But you must (1) create your characters' emotions in your own mind, then (2) effectively describe those emotions on paper. From that point, (3) your audience has to read words and finally (4) re-form the images of those emotions in their own minds. It is so easy for those emotions to lose their depth of meaning in any one of these steps. One thing is certain. Considering how far removed your readers are, if you want them to feel the passions of your characters in all their glory, you—being at the starting point—will need to feel these passions as fully as possible yourself.

But how to do this? How to plumb the depths of the well of emotions within you, rather than merely skim the surface?

Once again we look to the art of Method acting to guide us. How does the Method actor believably portray the unique emotions and desires of different characters, particularly when a character faces conflict that the actor has never faced? Answer: by tapping into his emotion memory.

Emotion memory was first spoken of by the French psychologist Théodule Ribot, who called it "affective memory." Stanislavsky explained this "affective" or "emotion memory" as the kind of memory that makes a person relive all the sensations he or she felt when faced with a certain situation. Emotion memory can fill a person anew with the feelings of that moment, even though these feelings may have long before sunk into the subconscious. These are memories in their most pure, distilled form. They are simmered by time just as a sauce simmers on the stove until excess liquid is gone and all that remains is potent, blended flavor.

A friend of mine once told me of baking a dessert on a hot summer day. She mixed all the ingredients, poured the mixture into a pan, and slid it into the oven. Then she went outside to work in the yard. When she reentered the house some time later, she was struck by a familiar smell wafting from the oven. The smell combined items she'd used in the baking—oranges and cloves and cinnamon. In an instant, that smell transported my friend to Christmas—the remembrance of oranges and apples stuck with cloves, bobbing in hot cider. That rich, sweet, heady scent filled her mind with scenes of celebrating the season with family: the joy of opening presents, the frustration of awaiting her turn in the bathroom, the biting cold of caroling house-to-house, the sadness of saying goodbye at the airport. All the emotions of the season in their vibrant colors, the deep meaning of the Christmas celebration—all these memories released themselves from my friend's subconscious, sweeping her in one instant from a hot summer kitchen to Christmas. Merely because of a smell.

Accessing Your Emotion Memory

Any one of our five senses, or any combination of them, can release vivid memories like the one above from our subconscious. The problem is, we can't count on such serendipitous moments to trigger the emotions we need to feel while writing a certain scene. As we all know, emotions have minds of their own. They are often fleeting, teasing, no more than vague, ghostlike impressions.

"Our artistic emotions," Stanislavsky told his students in *An*

Actor Prepares, "are at first as shy as wild animals, and they hide in the depths of our souls. If they do not come to the surface spontaneously, you cannot go after them and find them. All you can do is concentrate your attention on the most effective kind of lure for them."

Because we need them, and they don't always appear at will, we have to learn how to access them. Through conscious effort, we can tap into our emotion memory, causing subconscious feelings to rise to the surface, much as a well-digger taps into a hidden spring, and suddenly fresh water bubbles forth.

When we learn to access our emotion memory, two wonderful results occur in our writing:

1. We can far more splendidly color the passions of those characters whose experiences are similar to our own.

   Sometimes we create characters whose main hardships are based on those we've faced in our own lives. Still, your character will encounter some situations that are different—or perhaps worse—than your own, and she will have a Desire and inner values that do not exactly match yours. When her passions must diverge from your own, tapping into your emotion memory will help you discover all the colors of her unique situation. This character can become far more than a mere carbon copy of your own experiences.

2. We can create characters who are completely different from ourselves—and perhaps even anathema to our own ways of thinking.

   Through releasing the sensations of your own experiences, emotion memory allows you a surprising glimpse into souls whom you may have thought you could never understand. You can then enlarge these "glimpses" until you create a complete portrait of a character.

As the previous sentence suggests, emotion memory is not the be-all and end-all of your ability to feel your character's passions. On the contrary, it is only the beginning. It is the seed from which your understanding of a character can grow. Just as a plant also needs soil and water, so you must place the seed of your own emotions in your fertile imagination and creativity. With this mixture of your own emotions and imagination, you can create *any* character you choose to create.

At the close of this chapter, I will show you how powerful emotion memory can be in helping you create a character different from yourself. But first, let's look at the steps to accessing your emotion memory in order to discover the passions of a character in a given scene.

1. Find an experience or emotion in your own life that is similar to that of your character.

   Sometimes this is easy. If your character is experiencing his or her first crush, you've probably been through that yourself. Or if your character is at the funeral of a parent, and you've lost a loved one, you know the depth of grief. But when our characters face situations outside the realm of our own experience, this step becomes a little more tricky. Then we need to search our own experiences for an *emotion* that reflects what the character is feeling. Remember, the emotion need only be a "seed" for the passions of your character. For example, if your character faces crushing guilt over causing someone's death, find a time in your own life when you have felt guilty. It could be a time from your childhood, and it could even be over some relatively minor issue. The circumstances aren't important and don't need to match the severity of what your character is facing. What *is* important is that you felt guilt.

   Years ago when I was single, I awoke suddenly one morning, thinking I'd heard a noise in my apartment. I'd been cold during the night and had burrowed down into the covers; the bedspread was over my head. I tensed, listening. Again, I thought I heard something—a footstep entering my bedroom. My heart turned over, scudded into panicked beats. *Pull down the cover!* my insides screamed. *See who's there!* I knew I must. I knew I needed to see what was happening, be ready to *move*, to jump from the bed and defend myself. But in that second, an amazing thing happened to my body. Every limb, every sinew locked up tight, and I could not move a muscle. *Do it!* my mind screamed—and still I could not move. Internally, I wrenched against myself, willing my arm to grasp the bedspread, willing my head to lift off the pillow. And then suddenly my arm lurched. I flung the cover aside, snapped my head toward the doorway.

Nothing. Absolutely nothing. Whatever sound I'd heard had been imagined. I felt quite foolish.

A moment later, when my heart had slowed to a normal pace, I realized I'd discovered an amazing truth. I'd discovered that a person really can be "frozen in fear."

That minor incident of imagined danger hardly seems comparable to a scene in which my character faces a real intruder and her very life is at stake. But, again, the circumstances aren't important. I was *frozen in fear*. That small, otherwise insignificant event in my life, no more than five seconds from start to finish, was a powerful experience of raw fear. When I need to, I can expand upon my emotion memory of that event to write believably of a character's fear—even if she's facing death.

2. Relive your own experience by telling it out loud to yourself.

Brace yourself. This is where the "getting personal" really begins. You may at first feel inhibited or even scared, depending upon the emotion. But this is not the time to hold back. Find a time when you can be by yourself and uninterrupted.

Tell your experience to an imagined, captive audience, relating every detail you can remember, using all your five senses, if possible. First describe the setting. Then describe your actions and emotions, one by one. Get up, move around if you like. Act out the events.

Are you reliving a moment of excitement? Tell your experience until your eyes shine with the memory. Are you reliving jealousy? Tell it until you feel the fire in your stomach. Loss? Tell it until you can feel the pain.

Don't stop to take notes to record your emotions. Just *feel* them.

3. Add any external stimuli that may help you relive the memories.

   Is there anything that might help you in the retelling of your experience? A picture? A certain object? A certain smell, such as a perfume? Music? Use anything you can to help release the memories.

4. Once you have connected with your own emotions, use them as the seed for those of your character.

   Just as you had to translate your own inner rhythm to actions of your character in chapter 5, here you must translate your past experiences of emotions into the unique passions of your character. This is the step in which all the rest of our secrets come into play. Once you connect with your own emotions, once you fully remember how fear or grief or joy feels, you need to blend this knowledge with everything else you know about your character. What are your character's action objectives in the scene, and how could these emotions translate into them? What is his inner rhythm, and how can he show it? If he's talking with someone, will he be honest about his feelings or will they be subtexted? Write your scene infusing all of these things. Your renewed memories of the emotion, plus all you know of your character, will blend together to create a vivid and believable scene.

Refilling Your Emotion Memory

With all this dipping into the well, how do we keep our own reserves filled? For as surely as water can run low, so can our emotion memory.

> Keep the resources for your emotion memory filled by watching others and, most of all, yourself.

Once again, we need to emulate our acting cousins by *constantly observing life*. Strong writing requires an intimate knowledge of humanity. The only way to gain that knowledge is to live life to its fullest and to watch and record it as though your very life depended upon it. In fact, your writing life does.

First, you can refill your emotion memory by watching others, mentally recording their actions and perceived emotions in certain situations. Perhaps you've never been in a non-injury car accident but have observed one. How did those involved react as they hurried from their cars? How did others act as they stopped to help? Even more important, how did you feel as you empathized with these people?

Second, you can watch movies and plays and read books—always with the goal of recording emotions. Third, and most important of all, you can watch yourself. Now that you're aware of the emotion memory within your subconscious, you can actively record your own feelings in a way that will keep them closer to the conscious level, more readily available when you need them for writing.

I'll confess something. No matter what I'm going through, no matter what my emotion, even in moments of greatest joy or sorrow, there is a little part of me that disconnects to float to the corner of the ceiling and observe. Whether I laugh or cry or sink to my knees in despair, this writer side of me looks on quite objectively—watching, recording, saying, "Hm. I'll have to remember this." If I don't feel her in the midst of my passion, I feel her only seconds later, scrambling to take it all in, to remember the emotions in all their colors.

Remember to watch your insignificant moments as much as you watch major events in your life. As we've noted, a seemingly insignificant experience can unleash a powerful emotion memory. In fact, only when we discover this truth can we employ emotion memory to its fullest.

Richard Boleslavsky, a director of the Moscow Art Theater, wrote a wonderful little book called *Acting: The First Six Lessons*. In his lesson on emotion memory he tells an aspiring young actress, "We have a special memory for feelings, which works unconsciously by itself and for itself. It is in every artist. It is that which makes experience an essential part of our life and craft. All we have to do is to know how to use it." These memories, however small, Boleslavsky continued, are "just waiting to be awakened. And what is more, when you do awaken them, you can control them in your craft. . . . You *command* them."

The young actress asks, "Suppose I don't find a similar feeling in my life's experience, what then?" Boleslavsky replies that anyone who has lived a normal existence has experienced to some extent all the emotions of mankind. The woman challenges him. Surely this can't be true. What if she must play a murderer? She has certainly never murdered anyone or even felt the slightest desire to do so. Hogwash, replies Boleslavsky. (My paraphrase.) Ever been camping when mosquitoes were around? he asks. Ever follow one with your eyes and ears, your hate spurring you on, until you killed it? The actress admits that she has. "A good, sensitive artist doesn't need any more than that to play Othello and Desdemona's final scene," Boleslavsky declares.

What a startling thought!

To show you firsthand the power of emotion memory, I want to lead you moment by moment through my own version of Boleslavsky's example. When I first read Boleslavsky's book, I never dreamed how important the example would become to me. Then years later, I set out to write my suspense novel, *Eyes of Elisha*, and found myself in the mind of a killer. Who, *me*? How could I possibly write, with any believability, a scene about a soon-to-be serial killer stalking his first prey? What did I know of such bizarre, sick behavior?

A lot more than I'd ever have guessed.

And so do you.

Follow me now through this scene and allow yourself to discover the powerful depths of emotion memory. You may not have experienced this exact situation, but chances are you've experienced one very similar to it. From the smallest, most insignificant moment of your life you can unleash the emotion memory needed to portray one of mankind's most heinous acts.

A Murderous Example

Finally, the time has come. The time set aside just for yourself, when your guests have waved goodbye after their weeklong stay. You are alone in the house and exhausted. You don't care that you have work to do. All you can think of is: The Book.

You were reading it, loving it before the guests came. But all during the week you could only catch bits and pieces of it after falling into bed each night, your eyes fighting sleep. Last night you managed to read for almost an hour. You only have fifty pages left, and you can't wait to see how it all turns out.

Your guests now gone, you make a beeline for the book, grasp it from your nightstand and hurry to the family room. There, your steps slow. You hesitate in the center of the room, biting the inside of your lip. This long-awaited time is too good to rush through, you think. You want to enjoy it, revel in it. You blink as an idea flits across your mind. Tossing the book on the couch, you head for the kitchen. You'll make your favorite hot drink to sip and savor as you read. Ah, that will really do it! The mere anticipation rolls comfort, contentment, across your shoulders.

You hum a little tune as you make the drink. Its wonderful aroma tickles your nose as you carry the hot mug into the family room and place it on an end table. You pick up your book, settle into the couch with a sigh. Smiling, you open the novel, slip out the bookmark and begin to read.

Your eyes glide over the pages, your muscles relax, your mind empties of all but the events in the novel. Once in a while you pick up your mug, sip your drink. The house is quiet save for the distant ticking of a clock in the kitchen. You wish this time would never end.

The scene you're reading heats up. Oh, no! The heroine can't do *that;* whatever will become of her? And what about her nemesis— you know he's still up to no good. Surely he'll leap from the pages any moment now, aiming his intended miseries at the characters you are cheering. You turn the page. Aha. There he is. Oh, but surely he won't—

A fly cruises across the room.

Your eyes flick at it distractedly, then back to the book. You continue reading, devouring the words. Oh, the passions. You can *feel* the scenes. They sweep you off your feet, transport you. You want to hurry and finish the story to see what happens; you want the story never to end. You're almost done with a chapter. The evil adversary is turning to the hero and heroine, opening his mouth—

The fly buzzes against the family room window, backs up, then buzzes into it again.

Your eyes lift with irritation from the page, first to stare unseeing across the room as you listen, then to blink into a narrowed gaze at the fly. He is annoying. He is large. He is disturbing your peace, your moment. You wish he would go away.

He buzzes, smacks the window repeatedly.

You pull your eyes back to your book. You continue reading, your forehead etched in a frown of concentration.

A few minutes pass. Purposely ignoring the fly, you finish the chapter. Oh, what a hook! What will happen now? You turn the page, eager to continue. Without missing a word you grope for the mug with your left hand, raise it to your lips. Ah, the drink's still warm.

You read on. The book's main secret is about to be revealed. You can sense it coming. You think you know, but you're not sure. You read on, swept here and there as your characters run for their lives. Now through a forest, now facing a raging river. How will they cross? The hero is too weak—

The buzz-against-glass abruptly stops. Zzzzzz. The fly cruises the room again. He circles your head. You wave him away, still reading. He circles once more, exploring, coming in for a closer look, invading your space. You whisk out a frustrated hand to smack him and miss. He circles. You glare at him now, your eyes following his route. Your mouth tightens; the muscles in your thighs tense. You tap a thumb against the page of your book, reading momentarily forgotten. The fly lands across the room on the television set. You poke your tongue under your upper lip as you stare at it, half daring it to move. It doesn't.

You inhale deeply. Shift your position. Your eyes return to the page, flitting until they find where you left off. Ah, yes, the river.

You start reading. Within seconds you are again engrossed in the story. The water is rising around the couple; their nemesis is closing in. You're still not sure of what he wants, what he will do when he reaches them. He is yelling something over the boiling waters, his voice fading in and out of the torrents. The heroine screams at him—

The fly buzzes from the television and right by you. The sound reverberates in your ears. Then stops. You swivel your head to see the fly crawling, feeling his way with his nasty little legs along the rim of your cup. Anger kicks across your nerves. Your arm flashes out and scares him back into the air. The buzzing resumes—right in front of your nose.

"That's *it!*" You throw down your book and push off the couch, seething. The ugly creature flies around the room—*your* room—like he owns the place. Who does he think he *is*, disturbing you like that? Can't you have even *one hour* of peace in your own house? After all the company and hostessing and work? Can't you just be allowed to read your book and enjoy yourself for *one lousy moment?*

Muttering, you swivel on your heel and head for the kitchen, in search of something, anything, to get rid of this creature once and for all. You grab a newspaper section off the kitchen table, roll it quickly, and pace back into the family room, smacking it against your open palm. The fly still cruises. You lurch to a stop, your head on a constant swivel as you follow his flight. From the corner of your eye you notice that your book has fallen shut on the couch. Fresh anger jags up your chest. *Now* that wretched beast has caused you to lose your place!

The fly lands on the coffee table. You stride three steps and bring down the newspaper hard. *Thwack.* The fly lifts into the air, buzzing even harder. You exhale loudly, cursing under your breath. You were too mad, moved too quickly. You'll have do this steady-like, smooth. Have to think before you move.

You draw up straight, standing perfectly still, except for your head, which still follows the fly's path. The newspaper rests in your palm. You like the feel of it, the deadly force it promises. Now if you can only sneak up on that fly. You even breathe quietly lest it hear you. You command control of your own body, centering your focus on killing the fly—nothing else.

You don't stop to think that the fly is merely foraging for food he needs to exist. It doesn't occur to you that he means you no harm, that he's probably seeking a way to get out of your house. You certainly don't stop to think he may have family, that he may be missed once he's dead. Such an absurd notion would not last one second within your brain. Who could *possibly* care about this disgusting creature? And even if someone did, he has invaded *your* space. He deserves to die!

The fly lands on the window. Your eyes narrow as one side of your mouth curves into a smirk. You are careful this time—oh, so careful. Stealthily, silently, you creep across the carpet. Your fingers tighten around the newspaper. You hardly dare breathe. Three more steps. Your arm begins to draw back. Two more steps. Your shoulder muscles tighten. One more step. You glide to a halt, eyes never leaving the fly. You swallow. Pull back your arm further, fingers whitening around the newspaper. Every sinew in your upper body crackles with anticipation. Then, like a launched rubber band, your arm snaps forward, the rolled newspaper whistling through the air. *Thwack!!* The force of the hit sends shock waves up your arm.

The fly drops like a stone.

Yes! You've *killed* him!

But wait. Do you go back to your reading? Oh, no, no. You're not ready to be done with this deed quite yet.

You stand there, breathing hard, eyeing the dead fly. Your arm lowers, your fingers relax their grip. A slow, sick smile twists your lips. Your head tilts slightly, your eyebrows rise.

"Hah!" The word echoes in the room, hard and snide. "That'll teach you!"

You survey your handiwork, gloating some more, vindictiveness and satisfaction swirling. The fly is such an ugly thing. Black, mangled, dirty. Couldn't even die with dignity. It lies there, trashing up your nicely painted windowsill. Your lip curls. How disgusting.

That fly deserved everything it got.

One thing's for certain, you tell yourself. If any other fly comes along, you won't waste precious time trying to ignore it. Oh, no, you've got the actions *down* now. Next time, one tiny buzz, and you'll be off that couch, newspaper ready. It'll be *so much easier* next time.

But enough of that. Suddenly, you must rid yourself of your victim. Its very sight nauseates you. Your tear off a piece of the newspaper, and use it to pick up the body—gingerly, being careful not to touch it. No telling what sort of germs and filth it carries. You walk into the bathroom, throw it into the toilet. Flush it down. Still, you're not quite through. You watch it swirl faster, tighter, until it finally disappears. You smack down the toilet lid.

Now you are done.

You take a breath. Where were you? What was going on in your life before you were so rudely interrupted? Ah, of course! Reading! You hurry back to your book, your mind already racing to remember where you left off. You throw yourself back onto the couch, pick up the novel, flip through pages, find your last-read sentence.

Two minutes later you are once again engrossed in the story, living and breathing along with the characters. Your house is so peaceful. Life is wonderful. You are happy.

You settle back, devouring the words. Reveling in your contentment. The fly is forgotten.

Almost.

Except for within that one part of you. That one tiny, separate part that cocks an ear, stands guard over your space, protectively listening for—almost *anticipating*—the buzz of the next fly . . .

 Study Samples

The two fiction scenes included in these samples are taken from Mark Twain's *The Adventures of Huckleberry Finn*. Interspersed with these scenes are excerpts from Twain's autobiography. The author's rich reminiscences about his life give us some wonderful glimpses into how he used his own emotion memory to create some of the most memorable characters and places in all of literature.

Before we look at scenes from *Huckleberry Finn*, consider first this excerpt from chapter XIII of Twain's *My Autobiography*, in which he writes about his childhood memories of being "at the farm" with his cousins. Twain uses all five senses in describing these memories, which he has obviously stored in his conscious mind for use again and again in his fiction.

FROM
My Autobiography
by Mark Twain

The life which I led there with my cousins was full of charm, and so is the memory of it yet. I can call back the solemn twilight and mystery of the deep woods, the earthy smells, the faint odors of the wild flowers, the sheen of rain-washed foliage, the rattling clatter of drops when the wind shook the trees, the far-off hammering of woodpeckers and the muffled drumming of wood-pheasants in the remoteness of the forest, the snap-shot glimpses of disturbed wild creatures scurrying through the grass,—I can call it all back and make it as real as it ever was, and as blessed. I can call back the prairie, and its loneliness and peace, and a vast hawk hanging motionless in the sky, with his wings spread wide and the blue of the vault showing through the fringe of their end-feathers. I can see the woods in their autumn dress, the oaks purple, the hickories washed with gold, the maples and the sumacs luminous with crimson fires, and I can hear the rustle made by the fallen leaves as we ploughed through them. I can see the blue clusters of wild grapes hanging amongst the foliage of the saplings, and I remember the taste of them and the smell. I know how the wild blackberries looked, and how they tasted; and the same with the pawpaws, the hazelnuts and the persimmons; and I can feel the thumping rain, upon my head, of hickory-nuts and walnuts when we were out in the frosty dawn to scramble for them with the pigs, and the gusts of wind loosed them and sent them down. I know the stain of blackberries, and how pretty it is; and I know the stain of walnut hulls, and how little it minds soap and water; also what grudged experience it had of either of them. I know the taste of maple sap, and when to gather it, and how to arrange the troughs and the delivery tubes, and how to boil down the juice, and how to hook the sugar after it is made; also how much better hooked sugar tastes than any that is honestly come by, let bigots say what they will. I know how a prize watermelon looks when it is sunning its fat rotundity among pumpkin-vines and "simblins"; I know how to tell when it is ripe without "plugging" it; I know how inviting it looks when it is cooling itself in a tub of water under the bed, waiting; I know how it looks when it lies on the table in the sheltered great floor-space between house and kitchen, and the children gathered for the sacrifice and their mouths watering; I know the crackling sound it makes when the carving-knife enters its end, and I can see the split fly along in front of the blade as the knife cleaves its way to the other end; I can see its halves fall apart and display the rich red meat and the black seeds, and the heart standing up, a luxury fit for the elect; I know how a boy looks, behind a yard-long slice of that melon, and I know how he feels; for I have been there. I know the taste of the watermelon which has been honestly come by, and I know the taste of the watermelon which has been acquired by art. Both taste good, but the experienced know which tastes best. I know the look of green apples and peaches and pears on the trees, and I know how entertaining they are when they are inside of a person. I know how ripe ones look when they are piled in pyramids under the trees, and how pretty they are and how vivid their colors. I know how a frozen apple looks, in a barrel down cellar in the winter-time, and how hard it is to bite, and how the frost makes the teeth ache, and yet how good it is, notwithstanding. I know the disposition of elderly people to select the specked apples for the children, and I once knew ways to beat the game. I know the look of an apple that is roasting and sizzling on a hearth on a winter's evening, and I know the comfort that comes of eating it hot, along with some sugar and a drench of cream. I know the delicate art and mystery of so cracking hickory-nuts and walnuts on a flatiron with a hammer that the kernels will be delivered whole, and I know how the nuts, taken in conjunction with winter apples, cider and doughnuts, make old people's tales and old jokes sound fresh and crisp and enchanting, and juggle an evening away before you know what went with the time. I know the look of Uncle Dan'l's kitchen as it was on privileged nights when I was a child, and I can see the white and black children grouped on the hearth, with the firelight playing on their faces and the shadows flickering upon the walls, clear back toward the cavernous gloom of the rear, and I can hear Uncle Dan'l telling the immortal tales which Uncle Remus Harris was to gather into his books and charm the world with, by and by; and I can feel again the creepy joy which quivered through me when the time for the ghost-story of the "Golden Arm" was reached—and the sense of regret, too, which came over me, for it was always the last story of the evening, and there was nothing between it and the unwelcome bed.

FROM

Huckleberry Finn
by Mark Twain

The Widow Douglas has taken in young Huckleberry Finn, saying she will raise him and make a respectable boy out of him, which is not exactly the kind of lifestyle Huck has in mind. During supper Miss Watson, the widow's sister, is "pecking" at Huck about turning his life around so he can go to the "good place" when he dies. By the time he retires to his room for the night, he is depressed and lonesome.

I went up to my room with a piece of candle, and put it on the table. Then I set down in a chair by the window and tried to think of something cheerful, but it warn't no use. I felt so lonesome I most wished I was dead. The stars were shining, and the leaves rustled in the woods ever so mournful; and I heard an owl, away off, who-whooing about somebody that was dead, and a whippowill and a dog crying about somebody that was going to die; and the wind was trying to whisper something to me, and I couldn't make out what it was, and so it made the cold shivers run over me. Then away out in the woods I heard that kind of a sound that a ghost makes when it wants to tell about something that's on its mind and can't make itself understood, and so can't rest easy in its grave, and has to go about that way every night grieving. I got so down-hearted and scared I did wish I had some company. Pretty soon a spider went crawling up my shoulder, and I flipped it off and it lit in the candle; and before I could budge it was all shriveled up. I didn't need anybody to tell me that that was an awful bad sign and would fetch me some bad luck, so I was scared and most shook the clothes off of me. I got up and turned around in my tracks three times and crossed my breast every time; and then I tied up a little lock of my hair with a thread to keep witches away. But I hadn't no confidence. You do that when you've lost a horseshoe that you've found, instead of nailing it up over the door, but I hadn't ever heard anybody say it was any way to keep off bad luck when you'd killed a spider.

Huck Finn's loneliness in the scene above mixes with a sense of the macabre as Twain weaves in ghosts and spiders and keeping witches away. Wonder how Twain may have come to mix the feeling of loneliness with such superstition? Consider the following two very different experiences from his past, separated by years and locality, that he likely blended together to help create the scene above.

FROM
My Autobiography
by Mark Twain

I remember only one circumstance connected with my life in [the house I was born in]. I remember it very well, though I was but two and a half years old at the time. The family packed up everything and started in wagons for Hannibal, on the Mississippi, thirty miles away. Toward night, when they camped and counted up the children, one was missing. I was the one. I had been left behind. Parents ought always to count the children before they start. I was having a good enough time playing by myself until I found that the doors were fastened and that there was a grisly deep silence brooding over the place. I knew, then, that the family were gone, and that they had forgotten me. I was well frightened, and I made all the noise I could, but no one was near and it did no good. I spent the afternoon in captivity and was not rescued until the gloaming had fallen and the place was alive with ghosts.

• • •

In the little log cabin lived a bedridden white-headed slave woman whom we visited daily, and looked upon with awe, for we believed she was upwards of a thousand years old and had talked with Moses. The younger negroes credited these statistics, and had furnished them to us in good faith. We accommodated all the details which came to us about her; and so we believed that she had lost her health in the long desert trip coming out of Egypt, and had never been able to get it back again. She had a round bald place on the crown of her head, and we used to creep around and gaze at it in reverent silence, and reflect that it was caused by fright through seeing Pharaoh drowned. We called her "Aunt" Hannah, Southern fashion. She was superstitious like the other negroes; also, like them, she was deeply religious. Like them, she had great faith in prayer, and employed it in all ordinary exigencies, but not in cases where a dead certainty of result was urgent. Whenever witches were around she tied up the remnant of her wool in little tufts, with white thread, and this promptly made the witches impotent.

Exploration Points

1. How might Twain's memory of being left alone when he was two have led to his memory of Aunt Hannah and her superstition?

   I think of two emotions that could have caused Twain to link these two memories. The fear he felt as a very young boy all alone in the dark must have been overwhelming. Most likely it lead to a feeling of helplessness. Fear and helplessness are also evident in the memory of Hannah, although in different forms. The young Twain made noise to scare away the "ghosts," while the old woman tied her hair in tufts to keep away witches.

2. How did the fusion of these two memories work to change Huck Finn's action objective in the scene?

   As he first enters his room, Huck is lonely and despondent from talking to the judgmental Miss Watson. His action objective is: to shake himself from his despondency. Here is where Twain's two memories seem to fuse. Every noise reminds Huck of his conversation about death with Miss Watson. The sounds of death lead him to think of ghosts, which turns his despondency into fear. When he kills a spider, his action objective immediately becomes: to protect himself from bad luck. The scene has taken on a whole new aura as he ties up a lock of his hair.

   If Twain hadn't fused the two memories from his childhood,

this scene of Huck alone in his room would not have been nearly so captivating, for Huck's action objective to protect himself from bad luck would not have arisen.

3. Is there a memory from your past that tends to lead to another memory of very different circumstances? Take a closer look at the two. What emotion links them in your mind? How might this linking be used in one of your scenes to prompt a character to unique action?

FROM
Huckleberry Finn
by Mark Twain

Huck Finn and a runaway slave named Jim are slipping down the river on a raft, watching for the town of Cairo. Jim is convinced that once he can reach Cairo he'll be a free man. Then they spot the lanterns of a town ahead.

Jim said it made him all over trembly and feverish to be so close to freedom. Well, I can tell you it made me all over trembly and feverish, too, to hear him, because I begun to get it through my head that he was most free—and who was to blame for it? Why, me. I couldn't get that out of my conscience, no how nor no way. It got to troubling me so I couldn't rest; I couldn't stay still in one place. It hadn't ever come home to me before, what this thing was that I was doing. But now it did; and it stayed with me, and scorched me more and more. I tried to make out to myself that I warn't to blame, because I didn't run Jim off from his rightful owner; but it warn't no use, conscience up and says, every time, "But you knowed he was running for his freedom, and you could a paddled ashore and told somebody." That was so—I couldn't get around that noway. . . . I got to feeling so mean and so miserable I most wished I was dead. I fidgeted up and down the raft, abusing myself to myself, and Jim was fidgeting up and down past me. We neither of us could keep still. Every time he danced around and says, "Dah's Cairo!" it went through me like a shot, and I thought if it was Cairo I reckoned I would die of miserableness.

Jim talked out loud all the time while I was talking to myself. He was saying how the first thing he would do when he got to a free State he would go to saving up money and never spend a single cent, and when he got enough he would buy his wife, which was owned on a farm close to where Miss Watson lived; and then they would both work to buy the two children, and if their master wouldn't sell them, they'd get an Ab'litionist to go and steal them. . . .

I was sorry to hear Jim say that, it was such a lowering of him. My conscience got to stirring me up hotter than ever, until at last I says to it, "Let up on me—it ain't too late yet— I'll paddle ashore at the first light and tell." I felt easy and happy and light as a feather right off. All my troubles was gone. I went to looking out sharp for a light, and sort of singing to myself. By and by one showed. Jim sings out: "We's safe, Huck, we's safe! Jump up and crack yo' heels! Dat's de good ole Cairo at las', I jis knows it!"

I says: "I'll take the canoe and go and see, Jim. It might-n't be, you know."

He jumped and got the canoe ready, and put his old coat in the bottom for me to set on, and give me the paddle; and as I shoved off, he says: "Pooty soon I'll be a-shout'n' for joy, en I'll say, it's all on accounts o' Huck; I's a free man, en I couldn't ever ben free ef it hadn' ben for Huck; Huck done it. Jim won't ever forgit you, Huck; you's de bes' fren' Jim's ever had; en you's de only fren' ole Jim's got now."

I was paddling off, all in a sweat to tell on him; but when he says this, it seemed to kind of take the tuck all out of me. I went along slow then, and I warn't right down certain whether I was glad I started or whether I warn't. When I was fifty yards off, Jim says: "Dah you goes, de ole true Huck; de on'y white genlman dat ever kep' his promise to ole Jim."

Well, I just felt sick. But I says, I got to do it—I can't get out of it. Right then along comes a skiff with two men in it with guns, and they stopped and I stopped. One of them says: "What's that yonder?"

"A piece of a raft," I says.

"Do you belong on it?"

"Yes, sir."

"Any men on it?"

"Only one, sir."

"Well . . . is your man white or black?"

I didn't answer up prompt. I tried to, but the words wouldn't come. I tried for a second or two to brace up and out with it, but I warn't man enough—hadn't the spunk of a rabbit. I see I was weakening; so I just give up trying, and up and says: "He's white."

Mark Twain had fond memories of the slaves he knew as a child. Here he tells of his relationships with them and his attitude toward slavery.

FROM
My Autobiography
by Mark Twain

All the negroes were friends of ours, and with those of our own age we were in effect comrades. I say in effect, using the phrase as a modification. We were comrades, and yet not comrades; color and condition interposed a subtle line which both parties were conscious of, and which rendered complete fusion impossible. We had a faithful and affection-ate good friend, ally and adviser in "Uncle Dan'l," a middle-aged slave whose head was the best one in the negro quarter, whose sympathies were wide and warm, and whose heart was honest and simple and knew no guile. He has served me well, these many, many years. I have not seen him for more than half a century, and yet spiritually I have had his welcome company a good part of that time, and have staged him in books under his own name and as "Jim," and carted him all around—to Hannibal, down the Mississippi on a raft, and even across the Desert of Sahara in a balloon—and he has endured it all with the patience and friendliness and loyalty which were his birthright. It was on the farm that I got my strong liking for his race and my appreciation of certain of its fine qualities. This feeling and this estimate have stood the test of sixty years and more and have suffered no impairment. The black face is as welcome to me now as it was then.

In my schoolboy days I had no aversion to slavery. I was not aware that there was anything wrong about it. No one arraigned it in my hearing; the local papers said nothing against it; the local pulpit taught us that God approved it, that it was a holy thing, and that the doubter need only look in the Bible if he wished to settle his mind—and then the texts were read aloud to us to make the matter sure; if the slaves themselves had an aversion to slavery they were wise and said nothing. In Hannibal we seldom saw a slave misused; on the farm, never.

There was, however, one small incident of my boyhood days which touched this matter, and it must have meant a good deal to me or it would not have stayed in my memory, clear and sharp, vivid and shadowless, all these slow-drifting years. We had a little slave boy whom we had hired from some one, there in Hannibal. He was from the Eastern Shore of Maryland, and had been brought away from his family and his friends, half-way across the American continent, and sold. He was a cheery spirit, innocent and gentle, and the noisiest creature that ever was, perhaps. All day long he was singing, whistling, yelling, whooping, laughing—it was maddening, devastating, unendurable. At last, one day, I lost all my temper, and went raging to my mother, and said Sandy had been singing for an hour without a single break, and I couldn't stand it, and *wouldn't* she please shut him up. The tears came into her eyes, and her lip trembled, and she said something like this—

"Poor thing, when he sings, it shows that he is not remembering, and that comforts me; but when he is still, I am afraid he is thinking, and I cannot bear it. He will never see his mother again; if he can sing, I must not hinder it, but be thankful for it. If you were older, you would understand me; then that friendless child's noise would make you glad."

It was a simple speech, and made up of small words, but it went home, and Sandy's noise was not a trouble to me any more.

Exploration Points

1. How were Mark Twain's attitudes toward slavery as a boy fused with his attitudes as an adult many years later to create the ambivalence within Huck Finn in the scene above?

   Twain does a masterful job of combining his fondness for certain slaves and his appreciation of the black person's qualities with the illogical teachings of his youth—that slavery was right. This culture in which Twain grew up is the same culture of Huck Finn, and the worldview of that culture threatens to transcend all that Huck feels as a human being who is trusted by another. Fortunately, at the end of the scene, Huck's friendship with Jim wins out, and he protects him.

   Twain plays on these ironies by having Huck struggle not with guilt over thoughts of turning Jim in, but with guilt over thoughts of *not* turning him in. Huck's struggle against the culture of that society portrays the horrible callousness and casualness of slavery far more than if his guilt had followed the different course.

2. If Twain had chosen to have Huck Finn turn Jim in, how might he have used these same emotion memories to build believable motivation within Huck for such a choice?

Twain could have focused more on his memories of being taught that slavery was right, even good. He could have focused on the anger and annoyance he felt as a boy toward the young slave who was always maddeningly singing. At that moment in his boyhood, Twain was mirroring the worldview of society—black people were meant only for serving white people; they were never to be free with their actions in a way that could annoy whites. That emotion of annoyance is the same that Huck could have felt if the scene were written with a different ending. He could have decided that Jim was an extreme annoyance because his very kindness and trust were making Huck feel guilty. Had Huck given into such a feeling, he'd have turned Jim in to the authorities, just as, when he was a boy, Twain went running to his mother—his authority—over the actions of the singing boy.

3. Review one or two of your scenes that seem flat and unexciting. What emotion memories can you employ to breathe life into the actions and feelings of the characters?

Moving On

The reminiscences of Mark Twain are a wonderful example of how rich our emotion memories can be, and how deeply they can serve us in "getting into character." Even though emotion memory is our final adaptation of Method acting techniques, we have hardly reached a finishing point in some linear process of discovering our characters. As you have seen, this process is not linear but circular, one technique cycling us back to all the others. A certain emotion memory may cause you to rethink a character's action objectives in a scene. Those action objectives may end up clarifying a trait or mannerism from your personalizing process, or they may drive your character to subtext his conversation. This conversation may lead to new colors of the character's passions, which in turn drive his inner rhythm in a certain scene. Your desire to portray that scene to its fullest will lead you to write with sentence rhythm and compression, and to delve as deeply as you can into your emotion memory for even more insight into the character's action objectives.

And on it goes.

The novelist's challenge of "getting into character" is indeed never-ending. Ultimate characterization is an art that requires our lifetime pursuit—a pursuit that rests upon fervent, continual studying and recording of the human condition. When we blend new observations with these techniques that we've borrowed from our acting cousins, we will continue to see fresh, vibrant life breathed into our characters.

Even more important, we'll learn about ourselves—

Which leads to greater understanding of our characters—

And the cycle goes on.

A Word about the Appendices

In Appendix A, I have listed other books on fiction writing for your supplemental reading as you continue in the lifelong journey of honing your skills. Some of these are considered classics necessary for every novelist's library. Some are broad in scope, and others focus on one particular aspect of fiction.

Rather than simply naming a book's title and author, I've included information about its content so you can select the ones that may be most helpful to you. And—most importantly for our purposes—I've noted which Secrets the material in each book best supplements.

"Supplements" is the key word.

The Secrets we've discussed here are unique enough to the fiction world that you will not find them mentioned—much less discussed—in other writing books. But that hardly matters. All of these books have something to offer as the authors present their own techniques for characterization, dialogue, plotting, and sentence structure. A book on dialogue, for example, may not talk about subtexting directly, but if you're struggling for more realistic conversation in your novels, such a book would certainly be a good one to consider reading.

One more thing to keep in mind: I don't claim that all of the teaching in these books will agree with me on every point. All the better, I say. It's healthy to read widely in your study of the craft, taking from the various authors those concepts that work for you and leaving the rest. Some of these books will serve mainly as background reference materials that you can use to help define your characters—*after* taking them through the Personalizing process.

For more teaching on the Method acting techniques upon which this book is based, take a look at Appendix B. It lists basic information about Stanislavsky's "ABC" books—*An Actor Prepares, Building a Character,* and *Creating a Role*—plus Boleslavsky's *Acting: The First Six Lessons,* then pinpoints what chapters in these books most pertain to our Secrets.

However, rather than merely reading a chapter here and there to learn more about a certain Secret, I urge you at some point in your studies to read all four of these books in their entirety. Study them at length, allowing the rich teaching and concepts of Method acting to simmer in your mind. The more you understand these concepts, the more you'll see how they can be adapted for your own use. As you continue to incorporate them into your work, you will be surprised at how powerful your fiction can be.

Additional Books on Writing Fiction

(Information refers to the most recent editions.)

Beginnings, Middles and Ends by Nancy Kress. Paperback, 149 pages, Writer's Digest Books (Elements of Fiction Writing), May 1999.
- **Secrets supplemented: Action Objectives**

Kress is the author of over a dozen novels and the winner of both the Hugo and Nebula Awards. She also is a regular columnist for *Writer's Digest* magazine.

Overall, this book teaches how to create and sustain dramatic tension and how to build to an effective conclusion. If you want to focus exclusively on story structure and what part your characters play in plotting your story this is a book worth reading. It is divided into three parts, aptly titled "Beginnings," "Middles," and "Ends." Part I discusses the opening scene with the "hook" of the first three paragraphs, the second scene, and early revision. Part II covers how to keep the story on track in the middle, characters at midstory, getting "unstuck," and motivation and change for characters. Part III looks at satisfying endings, the last scene, the last paragraph, and the final sentence.

Building Believable Characters by Marc McCutcheon. Paperback, 282 pages, Writer's Digest Books, March 1996.
- **Secrets supplemented: Personalizing**

McCutcheon is the author of numerous reference books for

writers, several of which, like this one, deal with facts and details useful in writing fiction.

This book consists primarily of lists and can serve as a resource of information to help you describe characters, once you have taken them through the Personalizing process. As McCutcheon puts it, *Building Believable Characters* is a "bona fide thesaurus . . . to jog your imagination and show you words you might not think of on your own." The lists include dozens of types of mustaches, beards, noses, names, colors, facial expressions and hairstyles, to name a few. A character questionnaire is also included, which may be helpful during the Personalizing process.

Characters and Viewpoint by Orson Scott Card. Paperback, 182 pages, Writer's Digest Books (Elements of Fiction Writing), April 1999.
- **Secrets supplemented: Personalizing, Coloring Passions, Emotion Memory**

A science fiction author and university professor, Card has won such prestigious awards as the Hugo, Nebula, and World Fantasy Awards.

This book is divided into three parts. Part I, "Inventing Characters," discusses the basic makeup of characters and where to get ideas for creating them. Part II, "Constructing Characters," talks about the various types of characters, how and why they change, and how to raise their emotional stakes. Both of these sections in their entirety are helpful as you take a character through the Personalizing process. For supplementary discussion regarding Coloring Passions, read Chapter 12, "Transformations," which focuses on how to present believable change within characters through proper motivation. Chapter 3, "Where Do Characters Come From?," talks about accessing your own memories and building upon them, much like our Secret of Emotion Memory.

Part III, "Performing Characters," discusses voice, the various points of view, and different ways of presenting the story. Although these are not aspects covered by our Secrets, they are critical to constructing a solid story.

The Complete Writer's Guide to Heroes and Heroines by Tami D. Cowden, Caro LaFever, and Sue Viders. Paperback, 300 pages, Lone Eagle Publishing Company, June 2000.

- **Secrets supplemented: Personalizing, Action Objectives**

This book provides an easy, structured approach to creating characters and their conflicts through explaining literary archetypes and how they interact with one another. These archetypes can be used to create main as well as secondary characters. The authors note, "Characters who fall within these archetypes have starred in story after story, entertaining and informing the human experience for millennia. Review of myths, legends, fairy tales, epic poems, novels and film reveals that the protagonists who recur in these stories fall into sixteen distinctive categories, eight each for the heroes and heroines." The authors also provide brainstorming ideas for character-driven plot development. Cowden and LaFever, both of whom are award-winning romance authors, bring a well-honed commercial sensibility to this reference, making it particularly helpful for those interested in genre fiction.

Creating Character Emotions: Writing Compelling, Fresh Approaches That Express Your Characters' True Feelings by Ann Hood. Paperback, 176 pages, Story Press, February 1998.

- **Secrets supplemented: Coloring Passions**

Ann Hood is the author of seven novels, all published by Bantam/Doubleday, and has written numerous short stories for major magazines. She has also taught in universities and at writers' conferences.

This book is divided into two sections. Part I, "Writing About Emotion," is a short discussion on the complexity of human emotion and how it is depicted in fiction. Part II, from page nineteen on, systematically covers thirty-six emotions, presenting bad examples of how to write them, followed by good examples (excerpted from published works). Each chapter ends with practical exercises for depicting that particular emotion.

This book makes an excellent supplement to our Secret of Coloring Passions, not only because of the range of emotions it depicts, but because it offers the "bad examples," which are often helpful to point out common mistakes to the beginning writer.

Creating Characters: How to Build Story People by Dwight Swain. Paperback, 198 pages, Writer's Digest Books, 1994.
- **Secrets supplemented: Personalizing, Action Objectives, Subtexting, Coloring Passions**

"Fiction grows from story people," says Swain in the preface. "This book is designed to help you bring such people into being. From it you'll learn barn-brush characterization. Subtlety you'll have to master on your own."

By "story people," Swain means interesting characters who care about something strongly enough that they are moved into action to obtain it. This "ability to care," Swain says in Chapter 1, is at the core of every character. Swain's discussion about this "core" of caring combines our "inner values" in Personalizing and the "Desire" of a character in Action Objectives. He moves on to discuss a wide range of aspects within characterization, including how to flesh out personalities, how to create offbeat or amusing characters, creating the character's inner and outer worlds, and dialogue.

Swain is an excellent writing teacher, and this book is well worth reading for a general understanding of characterization. The "subtlety" that he leaves for novelists to master can then be sought through applying the Secrets learned here.

Creating Fiction: Instruction and Insights by Teachers of the Associated Writing Programs by Julie Checkoway, editor. Paperback, 294 pages, Story Press, 1999.
- **Secrets supplemented: Personalizing, Action Objectives, Restraint and Control**

Associated Writing Programs is a nonprofit organization founded in 1967 that includes almost 300 writing programs and conferences. All of the teachers who contributed to this book are accomplished novelists and/or short story writers.

Chapters teach character development (minor characters, using setting to deepen characterization, difficult characters); point of view; plot, structure, and narrative (sequencing, describing and withholding, beginnings and endings); style and voice, and revising. Each chapter contains writing exercises, with an additional forty at the end of the book.

Description by Monica Wood. Paperback, 171 pages, August 1999.
- **Secrets supplemented: Restraint and Control**

In this book, Wood, a novelist and award-winning short story writer, teaches in detail how to awaken readers' five senses by using creative description that advances story, and how to edit out ineffective description. She also discusses description as it relates to style, mood, and point of view, using excerpts of various novelists' work as examples. The book includes dos and don'ts, lists of descriptive alternatives for common verbs and nouns, and tips for editing. This book is helpful to both beginning and more advanced writers as they hone the technique of Restraint and Control.

Dynamic Characters: How to Create Personalities That Keep Readers Captivated by Nancy Kress. Hardcover, 272 pages, Writer's Digest Books, July 1998.
- **Secrets supplemented: Personalizing, Action Objectives, Subtexting, Coloring Passions, Inner Rhythm**

This excellent book on characterization supplements five of our seven Secrets. It focuses on how to create strong characters that will act as the driving force for your story, from beginning to satisfying end. Its chapters are divided into three sections. Part I covers external characterization, including what characters do, names, characterization through dialogue, keeping character description to a manageable level, and basing characters on real people. Part II discusses internal characterization, including attitude, making characters' thoughts clear, overcoming assumptions about characters, using dreams and newscasts to enhance characterization, bad guys, and unsympathetic protagonists. Part III looks at the issues of conflict, violence, point of view, secondary characters, character change as a strong element of plot, basing plot on real life events, and archetypal characters. If you're looking for a book with depth and insight into character-building, this is well worth the money.

Fiction Writer's Handbook by Hallie and Whit Burnett. Paperback, 200 pages, HarperPerennial, January 1993.

- **Secrets supplemented: Personalizing, Action Objectives, Sub-texting, Coloring Passions**

The Burnett team, co-editors of the first incarnation of *Story* magazine, published the first works of noted authors such as Norman Mailer, J. D. Salinger, Tennessee Williams, and Truman Capote.

This wide-ranging book, whose preface was written by Norman Mailer, was first published in 1975 and is still a popular seller. The section on elements of fiction discusses plot, narrative, characterization, dialogue, style, sources of material, beginning the story, roughing out chapters, suspense, emotional color, and rewriting—elements that correspond with several of our Secrets. Excerpts from published works serve as examples for each technique.

The First Five Pages: A Writer's Guide to Staying Out of the Rejection Pile by Noah T. Lukeman. Paperback, 208 pages, Fireside, January 2000.

- **Secrets supplemented: Personalizing, Action Objectives, Restraint and Control**

Lukeman has years of experience as a literary agent. His clients include Pulitzer Prize nominees, *New York Times* best-selling authors, Pushcart Prize recipients, and American Book Award winners.

"After reading more than 15,000 manuscripts in the last few years alone," Lukeman says, "I couldn't help but notice that many writers—from Texas to Vermont to Japan—fall prey to the exact same mistakes." *The First Five Pages* looks at these common pitfalls, including the use of too many adjectives/adverbs, unrealistic dialogue, weak opening hook, forced or flat metaphors/similes, poor characterization and setting, uneven pacing, and lack of progression. In each chapter he identifies the problem and presents solutions, using examples to further the teaching, and includes exercises.

How to Grow a Novel: The Most Common Mistakes Writers Make and How to Overcome Them by Sol Stein. Hardcover, 288 pages, St. Martin's Press, December 1999.

- **Secrets supplemented: Personalizing, Action Objectives, Subtexting, Coloring Passions**

  Stein, the author of nine novels, including the best-selling *The Magician*, has also edited major writers such as James Baldwin, Jack Higgins, and Elia Kazan, and has taught many others how to write through his practical, specific techniques. He has lectured on creative writing at Columbia, Iowa, UCLA, and the University of California at Irvine.

  How to Grow a Novel continues the teachings presented in the immensely popular *Stein on Writing* (see page 202), using examples from Stein's coaching of many authors, from newcomers to bestsellers. Beginning and experienced novelists alike will benefit from reading this book and its companion. Here, Stein teaches how to write fiction full of "tension, suspense, anxiety, and pleasure," which, he says, are "all the things readers hope for when they turn to a novel." He includes insightful chapters on characters, plot, dialogue, point of view, and revising. Chapter 2 provides an excellent view of the nature of conflict, which, he explains, can be just as compelling in the form of quiet dialogue as in high action. Chapter 13 is an interesting look at revision, focusing not only on its potential to enhance a novel, but also on its pitfalls.

How to Write a Damn Good Novel by James Frey. Hardcover, 174 pages, St. Martin's Press, October 1987.

- **Secrets supplemented: Personalizing, Action Objectives, Subtexting**

  Frey is the author of nine novels and an Edgar Award nominee as well as a popular writing instructor.

  Here, he discusses a wide variety of points to consider in writing a novel. He explains how to make characters "sizzle" and be "round" instead of "flat," how to create fictional biographies, how to interview characters, and how to avoid stereotypes—all techniques that supplement the Personalizing process. He also discusses the "ruling passion" as the core of the character, which is similar to the Desire discussed in our Secret of Action Objectives. His chapter titled "The Fine Art of Dialogue" focuses on his four-point checklist, which says that dialogue should be "in conflict, indirect, clever and colorful." The "indirect" aspect is similar to Subtexting. This book contains helpful points for beginning writers as well as those with experience.

How to Write a Damn Good Novel II by James Frey. Hardcover, 161 pages, St. Martin's Press, April 1994.
- **Secrets supplemented: Personalizing, Action Objectives, Subtexting**
This title expands on the book above, discussing concepts such as developing "truly memorable" characters, creating suspense, premise, narrative voice, and writing with passion. It includes examples from a broad range of fiction.

How to Write and Sell Your First Novel by Oscar Collier, with Frances Spatz Leighton. Paperback, 264 pages, Writer's Digest Books, 1997.
- **Secrets supplemented: Personalizing, Action Objectives**
Collier is a former senior editor of the Prentice-Hall trade book division and has twenty-five years of experience as a literary agent. Leighton is the coauthor of over thirty books.

Only the first half of this book is applicable to Personalizing and Action Objectives techniques; the second half examines the early careers of twenty-three well-known authors. Part I explores major fiction genres as well as the four ingredients of effective fiction (compelling plot; grabber opening; successful ending; and a middle that keeps readers hoping, guessing, and involved).

The Novelist's Essential Guide to Crafting Scenes by Raymond Obstfeld. Paperback, 218 pages, Writer's Digest Books, 2000.
- **Secrets supplemented: Action Objectives**
Obstfeld is the author of twenty-seven novels in a wide variety of genres, which in total have been translated into eleven languages.

In this book, Obstfeld focuses exclusively on writing scenes:

what a scene is, how to start one, appropriate length, point of view, setting, editing, plot and theme, making payoff scenes work, various genre scenes (such as action, suspense, comic, romantic, and sex scenes), structure, and revision.

Scene and Structure by Jack M. Bickham. Paperback, 168 pages, Writer's Digest Books (Elements of Fiction Writing), reprinted edition April, 1999.

- **Secrets supplemented: Action Objectives**

Bickham is the author of over eighty novels and a former creative writing professor who has taught thousands through his classes, seminars, and *Writer's Digest* magazine articles.

Using examples from his own works, including *Dropshot* and *Tiebreaker*, Bickham demonstrates how to build a framework for a novel. He discusses scene length, cause and effect, stimulus and response, how to build a classic scene, scene sequels, pacing, how to liven up a chapter, how to write a book with multiple points of view, and more.

Self-Editing for Fiction Writers by Renni Browne and Dave King. Paperback, 240 pages, HarperCollins, reprint edition March 1994.

- **Secrets supplemented: Personalizing, Action Objectives, Subtexting, Restraint and Control**

Renni Browne served as a senior editor for many years with William Morrow and other publishers. In 1980 she left mainstream publishing to found The Editorial Department, now headquartered in Tucson, Arizona. David King, a contributing editor for *Writer's Digest*, owns and operates the Dave King Editorial Service in Ashfield, Massachusetts.

This highly acclaimed book teaches the techniques that professional editors employ to refine a manuscript for publishing. It discusses the concepts of showing vs. telling, characterization and exposition, dialogue, beats, paragraph breaks, interior monologue, proportion, voice, and sophistication. The authors use numerous examples from classic literature (such as *The Great Gatsby*) to show

how these passages could have been improved through the use of their editing techniques. Exercises are included at the end of each chapter, as are checklists for use in editing your own manuscripts.

Stein on Writing by Sol Stein. Paperback, 320 pages, Griffin Trade Paperback, January 2000.

- **Secrets supplemented: Personalizing, Action Objectives**

Stein's material in this popular book is divided into seven parts: "Essentials," "Fiction," "Fiction and Nonfiction," "Nonfiction," "Literary Values in Fiction and Nonfiction," "Revision," and "Where to Get Help." In the sections about fiction writing, he discusses swift characterization, the basics of plot, developing drama in plots, creating scenes, and more. This material dovetails with Stein's other title, *How to Grow a Novel* (see page 199), and complements the Secrets of Personalizing and Action Objectives well.

Techniques of the Selling Writer by Dwight Swain. Paperback, 330 pages, University of Oklahoma Press, 1973.

- **Secrets supplemented: Personalizing, Action Objectives, Coloring Passions, Restraint and Control, Inner Rhythm**

Originally published in 1965, this book is still considered one of the major works on fiction writing. Swain's ten chapters are so tightly packed with information that you'll need to read this book through more than once. Chapter 2, "The Words You Write," goes hand in hand with Restraint and Control. Chapter 3, "Plain Facts About Feelings," complements both the Secrets of Coloring Passions and Inner Rhythm. Chapters 4 through 6 discuss conflict and story structure, supplementing Action Objectives. Chapter 7, "The People in Your Story," combines excellently with Personalizing.

The 38 Most Common Fiction Writing Mistakes (And How to Avoid Them) by Jack M. Bickham. Paperback, 118 pages, Writer's Digest Books, 1997.

- **Secrets supplemented: Personalizing, Action Objectives, Restraint and Control**

Bickham's book is divided into thirty-eight chapters, one for each "mistake." Each one is titled in the form of a "don't," for example, "Don't Show Off When You Write." Other topics covered are story beginnings, description ("Don't Describe Sunsets"), conflict, characterization, character background and motivation ("Don't Write About Wimps"), cause and effect, viewpoint, scene structure, story direction, plot ideas, and when to stop the story. The chapters are short and therefore do not go into much detail about any one aspect. Nevertheless, the beginning writer will find numerous gems of knowledge here.

Word Painting: A Guide to Writing More Descriptively by Rebecca McClanahan. Hardcover, 256 pages, Writer's Digest Books, March 1999.
- **Secrets supplemented: Restraint and Control**
An award-winning writer, poet, and teacher, McClanahan uses her experience with poetry to teach others how to deepen their writing through enriched word choice. She discusses how to use description in bringing characters to life, plotting, pacing, setting, point of view, and portraying senses. Practical exercises are included at the end of each chapter. This book provides a helpful tool for self-editing.

The Writer's Guide to Character Traits by Linda N. Edelstein. Hardcover, 288 pages, October 1999.
- **Secrets supplemented: Personalizing**
Dr. Edelstein, a practicing psychologist for more than 15 years, is associate professor at the Chicago School of Professional Psychology and the author of two books on psychology.
She calls this book a "friendly reference" for novelists who want "to create believable characters and need accurate information about personality and behavior." She includes over 400 lists of personality styles and types, which arise from background experiences based on child development, romance, handicaps, psychological disorders, and criminality, to name a few. The book features hundreds of quick lists, including a large index of character/trait cross-referencing.

Writing and Selling Your Novel by Jack M. Bickham. Hardcover, 208 pages, Writer's Digest Books, October 1996.

- **Secrets supplemented: Personalizing, Action Objectives**

Written before *Scene and Structure*, this book teaches writers effective work habits, how to build strong beginnings and endings, character development, and plot and scene structure, plus how to revise and tailor a novel for a competitive book market. Exercises are included.

Writing Dialogue by Tom Chiarella. Paperback, 176 pages, Writer's Digest Books, February 1998.

- **Secrets supplemented: Subtexting**

Chiarella, a professor at Depauw University in Indiana, is the author of a book of short stories, *Foley's Luck,* and is a contributing editor to *Esquire* magazine.

In the introduction, Chiarella states that the objective of this book is to help novelists "relearn listening" in order to create more effective dialogue in their stories. Some of the topics covered are direction of dialogue, compression, the use of silence, and dialogue as a way to create stories. Chiarella's technique of "compression" goes hand in hand with our Secret of Subtexting.

Writing Fiction: A Guide to Narrative Craft by Janet Burroway. Paperback, 384 pages, Addison-Wesley Publishing Company, fifth edition July 1999.

- **Secrets supplemented: Personalizing, Action Objectives, Coloring Passions, Restraint and Control**

In addition to this title, veteran author Burroway has also written novels, plays, poetry, and a children's book. Specializing in creative writing (fiction and drama) and modern British literature, she has taught at both Cambridge and the Yale School of Drama.

In this hefty book, Burroway covers a wide range of topics, including the writing process; basics of story structure (conflict, crisis, resolution); voice, rhythm, characterization (including rounded versus flat characters); dialogue, mood; point of view; theme; and descriptive techniques such as metaphor and simile.

Writing the Breakout Novel by Donald Maass. Hardcover, 264 pages, Writer's Digest Books, 2001.

- **Secrets supplemented: Personalizing, Action Objectives, Coloring Passions**

As President of Donald Maass Literary Agency in New York, Maass has represented numerous best-selling authors, including Anne Perry and James Patterson. He is also the author of seventeen novels.

Maass's well-honed experience with fiction is evident as he discusses the common elements of all breakout novels, covering a variety of topics, from premise and plotting to multiple viewpoints. As its title suggests, *Writing the Breakout Novel* is not for beginning novelists, but for those seeking to hone their techniques in whatever genre they write. The chapter on characters is particularly insightful as Maass discusses some issues that other writers do not, such as dark protagonists and advanced character relationships. He uses excerpts from the works of many best-selling authors, plus checklists at the end of each section for review.

Writing the Natural Way: Using Right-Brain Techniques to Release Your Expressive Power by Gabriele Rico, Ph.D. Paperback, 262 pages, J. P. Tarcher, revised edition May 2000.

- **Secrets supplemented: Emotion Memory**

Dr. Rico is a popular lecturer and a professor of English and Creative Arts at San Jose State University. She developed her technique of "clustering," which is based on her studies of split-brain research and creativity in the writing process, as part of her doctoral dissertation at Stanford University.

In this book, Dr. Rico focuses on the mental processes behind creative writing. Through her technique of "clustering," she teaches authors how to free themselves from their inner critics and tap into what's already inside them in order to write passionately and believably.

Writing the Novel: From Plot to Print by Lawrence Block. Paperback, 204 pages, Writer's Digest Books, 1985.

- **Secrets supplemented: Personalizing, Action Objectives, Restraint and Control, Emotion Memory**

An award-winning author of mystery novels, Block is past president of the Mystery Writers of America and Private Eye Writers of America.

Block tackles a wide variety of issues in this book, which is helpful to novelists within all genres. The fifteen chapters include developing plot and characters, outlining, capitalizing on one's own experiences, descriptive passages, point of view, length, rewriting, getting published, and moving on to the next book.

Zen in the Art of Writing by Ray Bradbury. Paperback, 159 pages, Bantam, 1992.

- **Secrets supplemented: Emotion Memory**

Bradbury is an internationally known, best-selling novelist and short story writer whose works include *Fahrenheit 451* and *The Martian Chronicles*. Included among his numerous distinctions are the Nebula, Bram Stoker, World Fantasy, and International Horror Guild awards. He has been writing for over fifty years.

In this wonderful little book, Bradbury presents a collection of ten essays, written over a period of thirty years. He says of them: "all echo the same truths of explosive self-revelation and continuous astonishment at what your deep well contains if you just haul off and shout down it." The essays contain his own experiences in creating his various stories, often focusing on where the ideas came from. In his early years, he wrote lists of nouns and "brief notes and descriptions of loves and hates," which in time helped him feel his way "toward something honest, hidden under the trapdoor on the top of my skull." Although Bradbury does not use the Method acting term "emotion memory," he certainly employs the concept.

Books on Method Acting by Stanislavsky and Boleslavsky

(Information refers to the most recent editions.)

An Actor Prepares by Constantin Stanislavsky, translator Elizabeth R. Hapgood. Paperback, 318 pages, Routledge/Theatre Arts Books, 1989.

This, the first of Stanislavsky's ABC books, presents his teachings through the narration of a fictional acting student, Kostya, as he and his comrades attend classes taught by the great Director Tortsov (a stand-in for Stanislavsky himself). *An Actor Prepares* focuses on the inner preparation of an actor as he explores the depths of a role. The book also discusses action, relaxation, concentration, and imagination.

Building a Character by Constantin Stanislavsky, translator Elizabeth R. Hapgood. Paperback, 308 pages, Routledge/Theatre Arts Books, 1989.

In this book, Stanislavsky's second, Kostya and his fellow students learn how to use what they have learned about the inner lives of their characters to create the characters externally. Stanislavsky covers topics such as dressing a character, expression, diction, intonation, perspective, and tempo-rhythm in speech and movement.

Creating a Role by Constantin Stanislavsky, translator Elizabeth R. Hapgood. Paperback, 274 pages, Routledge/Theatre Arts Books, 1989.

In Part I, Stanislavsky speaks as himself as he takes the reader through preparation of roles from one of Russia's most popular plays, Griboyedov's *Woe from Wit*. In Part II, he returns to the fictional narration of Tortsov and his acting class as they prepare roles from Shakespeare's *Othello*. As the acting class prepares these roles, Stanislavsky revisits the techniques and concepts from his first two books, demonstrating how they are put into action to bring characters to life.

Acting: The First Six Lessons by Richard Boleslavsky. Hardcover, 134 pages, Routledge/Theatre Arts Books, 1987.

This little book can be read in an hour, but it takes a lifetime to absorb. Richard Boleslavsky, born in Poland and educated in Russia, began training at the Moscow Art Theatre in 1906 and remained a member of Stanislavsky's company until 1920. Later, he came to America, directing both Broadway plays and Hollywood films.

As with Stanislavsky's books, Boleslavsky's lessons are taught in a fictional setting, with "The Creature," a young female acting student, posing questions to the teacher. The lessons/chapters are: "Concentration," "Memory of Emotion," "Dramatic Action," "Characterization," "Observation," and "Rhythm." Boleslavsky set these chapters months and sometimes years apart in "The Creature's" study of acting, knowing the growth that would need to occur within her between the lessons.

Chapters That Correspond to Each Secret

BOOKS ON METHOD ACTING

SECRET	*An Actor Prepares*	*Building a Character*	*Creating a Role*	*Acting: The First Six Lessons*
Personalizing	Chapter 2: "When Acting Is Art" Chapter 3: "Action"	Chapter 1: "Toward a Physical Characterization" Chapter 2: "Dressing a Character" Chapter 3: "Characters and Types"		The Fourth Lesson: "Characterization"
Action Objectives	Chapter 7: "Units and Objectives" Chapter 11: "Adaptation" Chapter 15: "The Super-Objective"		Part I, Chapter 2: "The Period of Emotional Experience"	
Subtexting		Chapter 8: "Intonations and Pauses"		
Coloring Passions			Part I, Chapter 2: "The Period of Emotional Experience— The Inner Tone" (subheading in Chapter 2)	
Inner Rhythm		Chapter 11: "Tempo-Rhythm in Movement" Chapter 12: "Speech Tempo-Rhythm"		The Sixth Lesson: "Rhythm"
Restraint and Control		Chapter 6: "Restraint and Control"		
Emotion Memory	Chapter 9: "Emotion Memory"			The Second Lesson: "Memory of Emotion"

Credits

Permission has generously been given to use extended quotations from the following copyrighted works.

From *Acting: The First Six Lessons* by Richard Boleslavsky, copyright © 1949 by Norma Boleslavsky. Courtesy of Routledge/Theatre Arts Books.

From *Color the Sidewalk for Me* by Brandilyn Collins, copyright © 2002 by Brandilyn Collins. Courtesy of Zondervan.

From *Eyes of Elisha* by Brandilyn Collins, copyright © 2001 by Brandilyn Collins. Courtesy of Zondervan.

From *A Question of Innocence* by Brandilyn Collins, copyright © 1995 by Brandilyn Collins. Courtesy of Avon Books.

From *Passing by Samaria* by Sharon Ewell Foster, copyright © 1999 by Sharon Ewell Foster. Used by permission of Multnomah Publishers, Inc.

From *Compelling Evidence* by Steve Martini, copyright © 1992 by Steve Martini. Courtesy of Penguin Putnam, Inc.

From *The Deep End of the Ocean* by Jacquelyn Mitchard, copyright © 1996 by Jacquelyn Mitchard. Used by permission of Viking Penguin, a division of Penguin Putnam, Inc.